The Great Gold Rush
A Tale of the Klondike

by
W. H. P. Jarvis

Double 9
BOOKS

The Great Gold Rush
A Tale of the Klondike
by W. H. P. Jarvis

ISBN: 978-93-61422-21-8

Published by

DOUBLE 9 BOOKS

2/13-B, Ansari Road
Daryaganj, New Delhi – 110002
info@double9books.com
www.double9books.com
Tel. 011-40042856

This book is under public domain

ABOUT THE AUTHOR

W. H. P. Jarvis, a renowned author and historian, is celebrated for his masterful depiction of historical events in his seminal work, "The Great Gold Rush." With meticulous research and captivating storytelling, Jarvis brings to life one of the most significant chapters in American history. In "The Great Gold Rush," Jarvis delves into the transformative era of the 19th-century gold rush, exploring the profound impact it had on the landscape, economy, and social fabric of the United States. Through vivid prose and vivid descriptions, he paints a vivid picture of the feverish excitement and relentless pursuit of wealth that characterized this tumultuous period. As readers journey through the pages of this masterpiece, they are transported back in time to the rugged landscapes of California and Alaska, where prospectors risked everything in search of fortune and adventure. Jarvis's evocative narrative captures the essence of the era, immersing readers in the sights, sounds, and emotions of the gold rush. "The Great Gold Rush" is more than just a historical account; it is a testament to Jarvis's skill as a storyteller and his ability to breathe life into the past.

CONTENTS

PREFACE

There is a freemasonry among Klondikers which rules that no tales shall be told out of school. If, therefore, this were an historical novel, if I were telling tales and seeking to escape censure by the subterfuge of changing names, I could hardly succeed. Let me take the case of Poo-Bah, for instance. The reader with a knowledge of the early days of Dawson accepting the story as historical, would fix as the original any one of half a dozen men indecently caricatured. But if he is told the character is a composite one, that it is the personification of Dawson graft, or, in other words, that it is the sum of a merger, he will understand and, I think, make no complaint.

Otherwise the story may be accepted as the author's best effort to convey a true account of the different phases of the world's most remarkable stampede. The stories of corruption among the officials in Dawson are those which a visitor would have heard on every hand, and at the present time there are many old-timers in the Yukon who will tell tales similar to the incidents I have introduced in my story.

When one of my characters speaks of the Dawson officials as petty larceny thieves and highway robbers, it is to be understood to be a sample of the phraseology in vogue at the time.

The different types of prospector I have attempted to portray are those I have met, lived with, and mixed with. Should it appear I have given too much space to the humble economies of the miner's life, I shall advance as my excuse the lack of our literature in this particular.

I have also made a humble attempt to establish the respectability of the miner. So much has been written to compromise him, and so many imaginations have drawn lurid pictures of his morals, I feel it his due.

In a general way the reader may accept anything in my story which has none other than an historical interest as being accurate.

I am indebted to the Rev. Archdeacon Macdonald, now of Winnipeg, for the story of his first discovery of gold. For the story of the discovery of Franklin Gulch I am indebted to Mr. William Hartz, who also furnished the accounts of the finding of gold in the Stewart River. These accounts have never before been written.

W. H. P. J.

Toronto, Canada.
January 1913.

CHAPTER I
THE FORTUNE-SEEKERS

Those who join the stampede to a new goldfield may generally be divided into two classes, the tenderfoot and the old-timer; otherwise, the novice and the experienced prospector.

The novice joins the stampede because he catches the "fever" — dreams dreams. The old-timer goes because the diggings he had last worked in proved of little good.

Were the sea-dogs of old — Drake, Raleigh, or Frobisher — born into the world to-day, their spirit would surely have impelled them to the mining camp, to seek fortune in the mountain fastnesses, and to wager years of effort on the chance of wresting from Nature her treasure stores.

On the steamship *Aleutian*, as she lay in the dock at Vancouver, British Columbia, one day in the March of 1898, there were many tenderfeet and a few old-timers. Amongst the experienced was John Berwick. About him surged the steamship's host of passengers, waving their arms, and yelling answers to the cheer that went up from the great crowd upon the dock-side.

He and his fellows were bound for the Klondike goldfields. Before them lay adventures, toil, and danger; the adventurous will ever draw the tributes of goodwill from the multitude staying at home.

The air was chill and damp; and the increased speed of the steamer as she passed from the harbour accentuated the effect of the breeze that blew against her, so that Berwick felt cold. He shivered, and half turned towards the door across the promenade; but the wavelets, flying by in their half-blue, half-grey ripples, fascinated him, and he lingered. Suddenly he was aroused — a hand was on his shoulder, and he heard a familiar voice say,

"Hullo, old chum!"

John swung round. He looked into the smiling face of his old-time mining-mate, George Bruce.

"George, by all the gods!" he cried. "Are you bound for the diggings, too?"

"Yes, and mighty glad to find an old mate. I told you, when you left Coolgardie, that you wouldn't stand civilization long, but had no idea of running across you in this rush."

The two turned and entered the saloon together. Neither mentioned it, but each knew that in the adventures before them their efforts and their fortunes would be joined. In the language of the Australian, they were mates, or, in the vernacular of their new surroundings, "partners."

George Bruce was tall and athletic, with golden hair. He was a jovial soul, blessed with a body of activity. He would go for the hardest work in a cheery way, and during the social hours of evening was the best of company. He was as liberal with his money and means as he was of good-nature.

The saloon was crowded with men, drifting about, staring at all they met, or talking in groups. On the lower deck dogs could be heard barking. The ship was tense with an atmosphere of excitement.

Berwick and his "pardner" went by a companion-way to the lower deck, where they found a passage-way to the fore-part of the ship, and so came to the presence of the canine choir. Big dogs and little dogs, of every breed and colour, were there. All grades of canine society were represented, from the big and well-fed St. Bernard to the mongrel snared in the slums. Dogs were a safe investment in the towns on the Pacific Coast of North America, and unscrupulous humanity was actively at work capturing them and getting them there.

The portion of the deck to which the dogs were relegated was also set apart for the baggage, which was piled in heaps in the middle. A dozen men were diving into kit-bags, extracting necessary articles or packing them away. The inspiration of the last few minutes in Vancouver had prompted many to purchase odds and ends which had been forgotten in the general outfitting.

A tall, angular man was attending to three dogs of an uncommon breed. Two of them were practically of the same size, which was that of an ordinary collie; the third was not so large. All had the same markings, black with tan about the face and neck, and a show of tan about the legs, but the hair on the two larger was longer than on the third. This couple also had bushy tails which curled over their backs, while the tail of the smaller dog was only a stump. John recognized them from their wolfish look as belonging to a Northern breed. George and he became interested.

After watching the dogs for a minute, John approached one of them and patted him, remarking to his owner, "Your dogs don't seem over-affectionate."

"No."

"They don't make much noise."

"These dogs never bark."

"Why is that?"

"Don't know; suppose it is because they have wolf in them; but they howl when the spirit moves them."

"Often?"

"Only when they are alone, and then generally at night."

The conversation was lapsing when the stranger turned and gazed at the mountains showing through the mist along the coast.

"Those mountains look kind o' cold," said he. "You fellows going inside?"

"Yes," answered John.

"Come from Australia?" The stranger had evidently been sizing them up. "There are a whole lot going inside from Australia, I hear."

"The only man I know on board is George Bruce here, my mate; but there is such a crowd about—there may be others!"

"The passes are already crowded—a whole lot of these fellows don't know what they are up against." The man shook his head with an aspect of melancholy.

"Been in the Klondike before?" Berwick asked him.

"Yes, five years ago. I came down from the River in '96, just before the news of Carmack's discovery reached Forty Mile, or else I would have been in on the best of it. The fellows sent me out word right after, but I didn't think the pay streak would hold, so didn't go in last year. But this spring I got so dead sick of civilization I just had to get away, although I don't think there's much chance of my striking it rich."

"Your dogs are Yukon dogs?"

"Yes, Malamoots. I brought them out with me just to kind of keep me from getting homesick, but they worked the other way. I took them back on the home ranch, and every time they set up a howl on winter nights I began to see the old Northern Lights sky-shooting overhead, and smell the bean-pot boiling, and I'd feel like getting down a hole to bed-rock somewhere and trying a pan of dirt. Besides, the folks outside, I don't like their ways; they ask a man so many fool questions. They all want to know why I ain't a millionaire. You see I've been up to Bonanza Creek where Carmack made his discovery, and where the rich claims have been discovered, a dozen times. We used to call it Rabbit Creek, and there were always a half-dozen moose or so mooching round, and we used to go shooting then."

"Didn't you ever try a dish of gravel?" asked George, for the first time entering the conversation.

The stranger looked at him, and evidently did not understand. John cleared the situation by saying, "I think what you call a pan we call a dish in Australia."

"Oh, yes, I've panned it often enough; but could not get more than a few colours to the pan of dirt. Fellows writing me say they go down through twenty feet of black muck before they strike the gravel and bed-rock. I was not looking for any proposition like that. How Carmack found out the gold was underneath I don't know."

The two friends bade their new acquaintance good evening, and returned to the saloon. All the seats were occupied, and there were yet groups of men standing about, but the excitement was less. They passed on to the smoking-room, at the fore-part of the ship. This was crowded, and the air thick. A large man in a white sweater was holding forth. He was stout almost to corpulency, and extended his fist excitedly in the ardour of his argument.

"I tell you, gentlemen," he was saying, "I come from the State of I-dee-ho. We have big mountains in I-dee-ho, with lots of snow on them in winter. I've lived among these mountains for twenty years, and I know what snow is; and you bet your life if there is one man who will get into the Yukon it is John Muggsley! Big Jack they called me back home. It's a big man who is needed on a trip like this, a fellow who can put a couple of hundred pounds on his back and walk off with it as if it were nothing. I tell you this is not a proposition for any tenderfoot to tackle!"

"Well," said another man, "I don't want any packing so far as I am concerned. I have two cows with me, both good milkers, and I will load my stuff on their backs and drive them over the pass. I can have their milk to drink, and when I get to Lake Bennett I'll kill them and sell their meat."

John and George had seen those cows. Poor cows! Poor man! So it was with a large portion of the passengers. With the excitement and the thirst for gold the most quixotic ideas had been developed. What the cows were to live upon en route had not yet been considered! Such is the haste with which an idea is acted upon when the gold-fever has seized its victim.

Others there were who had machine-propelled devices designed to travel over ice and snow, or on dry land. These machines were manufactured and sold by keen-witted salesmen to the inexperienced and confiding.

After dinner, that first evening out of port, John and George fell into conversation with the owner of the Malamoots. They had seized two of the cots erected in the saloon; and their new friend, seeing them, had taken one next to them. His greeting was friendly.

"Well, gentlemen, getting located?"

"Yes."

"Good act!"

The three were soon in deep conversation, discussing gold-mining as prosecuted in Australia and in the Yukon. After an hour or two they strolled forward between the cots, stepping over sacks and bags and articles of clothing spread upon the floor. They passed several tables at which games of cards were being played.

"The tin-horns are getting down to business," remarked the stranger.

"What are they playing?" asked George.

"Black Jack, the great game for the tenderfoot. It is so easily learned, so easy to cheat at, too; and these greenhorns will get robbed-blind."

"Their eyesight will be improved by the loss of their money," remarked John.

"A fool never learns," said the stranger.

They entered the smoking-room, and found Muggsley still holding forth, "Gentlemen, you just watch me and see how soon I get over these here mountains. It's experience that counts in this kind of work."

The man who had the cows, and he who was the proud possessor of the Klondike ice-locomotive were listening with some disdain; but the dozen other listeners were open-mouthed in envy and astonishment at wonderful Muggsley.

The three passed out on deck. The wind was chill, a frizzle was in the air, and the waves, breaking in dull phosphorescence against the bow of the ship, looked sickly and uncanny through the blackness. "A dangerous coast—the insurance rate for ships travelling this route is fifteen per cent.," remarked the stranger.

John Muggsley was still shaking his fist vociferously in the faces of his listeners as the party returned from deck to seek their beds.

"Good-night, you fellows. Glad I met you. My name's Hugh Spencer," the stranger said, as he settled in his cot.

"The same to you!" answered the others.

The freemasonry of the gold-seeker holds throughout the world, and its handshake is honest. Three gold-seekers have been introduced to the reader in this chapter; and these pages will tell something of what befell them in what was probably the most spectacular gold-rush in the history of the world.

John Berwick, who is by way of being our hero, shall have a chapter to himself.

CHAPTER II
JOHN BERWICK

Like most men whose success in life is largely the whim of fortune, John Berwick had for years accepted her rulings without protest, and regarded passing little incidents as signs of her influence.

One night in the December preceding his setting out for the Klondike, he was lying in his bunk on Judas Creek—one of the innumerable streams in British Columbia in which colours of gold, otherwise "prospects" could be found—reading a month old newspaper that a trapper, who had passed the previous night with him, had brought from the settlement, and in its columns had found an item of news telling of the recent rich discoveries in the Yukon. He read the paragraph carefully again and again, striving to separate exaggeration from truth, and to satisfy himself that there was truth in it.

By the camp stove sat Joe, the French-Canadian whom he employed, smoking and gazing at the glow of the fire with stolid and witless eyes. He would sit thus for hours; to a man of Berwick's temperament he was a satisfactory companion. On the Claim things had gone none too well. True, by great effort they had reached bed-rock at thirty feet, and were beginning to cross-cut in search of a pay-streak. There was certainly little gold in the gravel on the bed-rock already uncovered, and the flow of water into the working was very great: indeed, as much time was taken in keeping the shaft free of water as in all their other works combined. And up to three days previously rain had been incessant, though relief was apparently at hand, owing to the frost that had succeeded. The earth had hardened; Judas Creek was already flowing in less volume, and the boulders in the stream were becoming massed with ice.

Berwick had been but a few months on Judas Creek, having essayed to try his fortune in Canada's most western province. Fortune meant much to him—for lack of it hindered his marriage with the one necessary girl, Alice Peel, the only daughter of Surgeon-Major Peel. This was one cause of his presence on the frontier: another was that he and his religion had "fallen out" years ago. His father had intended him for the Church, and here he was....

"The Creek is falling rapidly, we can hardly hear it now," remarked John.

"Dat's so," was Joe's reply. He was laconic.

John's thoughts went back to his prospects. Much of his small capital had gone into the works. Joe was not in love—he had no capital save his strength of body, and his religion was negligible. When first this French-Canadian had arrived in British Columbia, and started work in a saw-mill, he had refused to work on Sunday, until the foreman told him that the devil never crossed the Rocky Mountains—which silenced his scruples. For sure, the Rocky Mountains were very high!

"I think we should empty the shaft to-morrow with seventy or seventy-five buckets."

"I guess dat's so."

Again Berwick relapsed into silence, and kept his mind on his many problems: had he or had he not better throw up his Judas Creek Claim, and strike out for the scene whence came these wonderful tales?

The volume of the Creek was diminishing with abnormal rapidity. For three days now frost had been upon the canyon, and the flying spray had frozen upon the boulders. The rushing, gurgling stream, falling over rocks and sunken logs, had during that time been sucking down bubbles of cold air, which sealed the fine ice particles to the river bed. For miles Judas Creek was lined with anchor ice, encasing the rocks with a coating, sickly, white, insidious. In the darkness the opaque ice seemed to shine out in phosphorescence; in fact, it threw back the light of the stars overhead, which seemed to have lowered themselves in the heavens—so bright and grand were they.

At a point a mile below the little pool where the nucleus of the mass now filling the river-bed had formed, a tree was stretched across the torrent. It had fallen into the stream above, and floated down until it jammed, holding back the current. The avalanche—as the thickening stream had now become—found this tree, and swept against it but a second, when it snapped. Now the flow of the river became a seething mass of ice and sticks—four feet high—travelling at the rate of several miles an hour, picking up all that came in its way. It passed the mouth of several tributaries, which lent it increase of force: still its speed quickened: the grinding noise increased— logs, sticks, masses of ice and great roots of trees appeared for an instant on its surface and sank again. Now the wave was five feet—now six feet high—broadening out, gaining yet in speed, still more effectually holding back the river's flow.

The gradual silencing of the river's roar was getting on the nerves of John Berwick, who was miles down-stream, far below the ice-flow. The river had tapered into a little rill.

When a certain noise has been a companion for days and days, and is suddenly stilled, a sense of uneasiness results, as when on a steamer the throb of the engine ceasing will rouse sleepers from their slumber. The slowing down of the torrent in Judas Creek made Berwick restless. He did not at first recognize what it was that worried him.

Joe also seemed as if he were not altogether proof against the spell; at last, he took his stare from the stove and looked around the cabin.

"I t'ink something pretty soon happen, by gosh!"

John stared at him; for Joe to volunteer a remark was unusual: it increased his employer's apprehension.

Berwick returned to his newspaper, fascinated by its news. A party of miners had arrived in San Francisco bringing much gold from some unknown region of the north. They called it the Klondike.

Would his Judas Creek Claim ever pay him for his efforts? What were his chances of fortune? Masses of gold or mountains of dust? He was in search of fortune—with a big "F."

His thoughts naturally drifted to the girl he wanted to marry. She was the daughter of luxury and wealth. He was just a prospector, no more in the eyes of Dame Fortune than the sturdy natural by the stove: in fact, experience had led him to believe that in the mining enterprise Fortune had a partiality for such men as Joe.

Berwick had been five years at the mining game. He had drifted from one camp to another: over America, to Australia, back to America. He had possibly become something of a cynic; certainly his mind had hardened with his muscles. He dreamed dreams. What would his lady say if she received a letter, saying he was again pulling stakes, and had left Judas Creek in order to avoid being defeated? He whistled, and shrugged his strong shoulders. He did not know!

He put some practical thoughts together. The Klondike was evidently in the North, far inland, in Canada. Could he withstand great cold? Yes, he could; he could endure and do anything as any other normal strong man could; and could go anywhere that was practicable to humanity. This was not vanity, not conceit, but just healthy self-confidence.

Should he pull up stakes and leave his Judas Creek Claim to the coyotes? As this question once more came to his mind, he was aware of the complete silence now outside, and letting his paper fall, bent his head to listen. Joe was listening also. Judas Creek was absolutely still.

Joe arose and opened the cabin door. His employer joined him there. There was no sound from the Creek; there was no Creek.

"By gosh! dat's funnee t'ing," Joe exclaimed.

"I certainly do not know how to account for it," said Berwick. He felt apprehensive.

They returned from the cabin door: Joe going to his seat by the stove, Berwick putting his bed in order for the night, when Joe jumped up and ran to the door again. A dull distant roar was heard.

"By gosh! By gosh! I got it! He's a river snow-slide what's coming. Quick, boss—quick! Get for hell out of dis! Pretty soon no more cabin—no windlass—no, no bucket, only water! No not'ing—all gone!"

The man began hurriedly putting on his boots, and instinctively his master followed his example, inquiring as he did so,

"What's that?"

"He's a river snow-slide, dat's all I know for to call him. A havalanche on wheels, all turn over—over—over! Him carry away everything, bridge, tree, dam—all sort of thing—everything go."

And as the sullen roar coming from the valley continued to increase, the appreciation of approaching danger spread from the one to the other. Berwick made haste and scrambled into his winter garb. Joe bundled together his personal effects, and some of the more valuable of the supplies in the cabin. Berwick did the same; out of the door they sprang into the night, and up the hillside, under which their cabin was built. Joe gave a sign when he considered they were out of danger. At once they threw down their loads and rushed back to the cabin. Grabbing another load they again sought the higher ground.

Meanwhile, the flood had broken from the canyon at the head of their little valley. The timber there had been largely cut, and over the rugged stumps the rolling mass spread, grinding, tearing up the weaker roots.

Berwick and his companion sat and watched their home going to destruction. Deliberately, it seemed, the mass of ice and water fell upon their workings. There was a loud crack as the windlass went down; and then the fury of water poured into their shaft. It was but for an instant. The flood tore against their cabin. Would the cabin endure the shock?

The answer soon came. There was a rending of timber; the cabin was pushed before the ice; and then it seemed to melt away, swallowed up by the flood. The lights went out. Lower and lower it sank, till the roof was touched by the surging ice. Then that, too, went under, and nothing but a fractured log or pole was left of the little home. John shivered.

The flood fell almost as quickly as it had risen, now that its work was proved effectual. Berwick turned to look at his man. Joe was already hard at work with an axe on a fallen tree, from which the chips flew.

. There was no doubt about it now. The Judas Creek venture was a failure: he could write it down as such. He had known many miners on whom Fortune had smiled; drunken swine, many of them, to whom money appealed only as a means to dissipation.

And he, to whom money—the price of his future home-happiness—meant so much!

Joe struck a match, applied it to a handful of birch-bark, and the flame sprang up.

By all the canons of his life, Berwick should have jumped into the fray and helped Joe make their camp; but, after all, it was only a little past nine o'clock.

Yes. Now he must throw up Judas Creek!

Joe laid twigs on top of the birch-bark and soon had a fire, to which he added larger sticks and logs. Then he cut down a fir-tree and made a bed, over which he spread the canvas of a tent and blankets. The night was perfectly clear, they would be warm and snug enough beside the fire.

Joe cut several more logs of wood and piled them near, after which he sat down upon the blankets, took off his boots and coat, rolled this into a pillow, and soon was asleep.

Berwick, sitting by the fire, watched far into the night. His fancy played about the flames, calling up scenes of his youth, and conceiving all manner of pictures of the miner's life in the sub-Arctic Klondike that was to be.

CHAPTER III
THE BEGINNING OF YUKON

No more wonderful system of navigation probably exists on the globe than that of the inland passage between Puget Sound and the Lynn Canal, at the head of which are the towns of Skagway and Dyea, the respective ports of the White and the Chilkoot Passes. For ten hundred miles the steamers plying along this route run behind the great barrier of islands, beginning with that of Vancouver and ending at Point Deception. In summer the trip is grand beyond compare; in winter it is full of gloom and awe.

As the ship travels northward the mountains grow greater, the narrow passages narrower, till they develop as canyons, cut only by other canyon-like passages to the sea, or by glacier-ridden valleys from the mainland, whose mighty burdens shimmer in the sunlight as they yield in torrents tributes to the parent ocean. In summer continuous light reigns in the latitude of Skagway, and the traveller entering this weird zone is moved by its uncanny beauty.

Winter was still on the land as the *Aleutian* ploughed her way northward, and the passengers saw the great walls of rock uplifting to the clammy mantle of low-lying clouds. Here and there Indian villages were passed and Indian graveyards, with flags flying from the stagings, raised six or eight feet from the ground, on which reposed the deceased.

The ship called at Wrangle and unloaded freight and passengers. "This town had a boom during the excitement of the Cassiar twenty years back," remarked Hugh Spencer to Berwick and Bruce, as the three stood on the deck and watched the bustle between the steamer and the wharf.

"Let's stretch our legs up the quay," said George. They went ashore. Squaws were sitting with baskets of their handiwork before them, doing a lively trade with the disembarked passengers. The sales made were mostly of moccasins in beads, and bark canoes adorned with porcupine quills of brightest colours. Hugh stopped before an old squaw and picked up a pair of large mittens with gauntlet attachments. They were made of canvas and lined with red flannel.

"How much?" he inquired.

"Dollar two bits."

"Give you six bits."

"All right."

"Better take a couple of pair each, fellows; there's nothing like them for the trail: look how big the thumbs are." So Hugh and his two companions bought the whole of the squaw's store.

"There's nobody knows how to make mitts for real cold weather like the Siwash. They make the thumbs good and big, so as not to stop circulation; and we'll have some cold weather yet before we get over the summit. But you have to beat the beggars down, as they always ask twice as much as they expect to get. Here we paid only seventy-five cents a pair for these mitts, and the squaw said she wanted a dollar and a quarter for them."

"Are these Siwash[1] Indians?" inquired John.

[1] Corruption of the French *sauvage*.

"Well, we call them Siwashes; but they don't like it. The real Siwash lives farther south, and the name, I believe, is one of contempt."

"They are different Indians from any I have seen on the plains," said John.

"Oh, yes, very different. I guess their only resemblance is that they are both good only when they are dead."

"You're pretty hard on them," was the remark of the good-natured John.

"Perhaps I am. You see, a tough outfit has been trading up here for years from down the coast; and before that the Russians were here—and they didn't put in most of their time building churches. They found a dollar's worth of hootch would get more from the savages than a dollar's worth of anything else; so they used whisky. The savage, when you find him without the cussedness taught by the white man, makes a pretty good citizen. He may be lazy, but he is honest; and perhaps his laziness is only due to the fact that he has always had a klootch[2] to do chores around, and has never been trained to the white man's ways of working; but let any fellow try following an Indian on snow-shoes for a couple of days, and his ideas soon change. He is not much good with a pick and shovel for sure; but he is A1 on the trail. Another thing about the Indian is that when one has grub they all have grub. This is the way of the Stick Indians inside, and you can cache your grub in their country or leave the things lying around, and they won't touch them."

[2] Squaw.

During the rest of the day John and his mates were in the company of Hugh Spencer, listening to his tales of Yukon life: the glories of the summer there, and the great cold of the winter, with the resources of the miners to keep from despair. He told them the traditions of the camps, and how the discoveries of '49 in California had been followed by others in Oregon, British Columbia, the Fort Steele district (Wild Horse Creek), Kettle River, Caribou, and, finally, in the Yukon.

"It wasn't a miner who was the first finder of gold in the Yukon; it was a missionary. But the missionary did not follow up this discovery, which makes a difference. However, I'll tell you the story, and it will let you see a little of Siwash nature in the telling of it.

"The Rev. Robert Macdonald, Doctor of Divinity and Archdeacon of MacKenzie River, was the first white man to find gold in the Yukon. Say! I ain't got much use for missionaries as a general proposition, but Archdeacon Macdonald is as white a man as ever lived, though he is east of the Rocky Mountains now. I guess the reason I don't like missionaries is that you can never do anything with the Siwashes, once a missionary gets hold of them.

"Well, the Archdeacon—he wasn't Archdeacon then though—drifted down the Porcupine, and took up his residence with the Hudson Bay Company people at Fort Yukon in the year 1862, which was a few years before I was born. You see the Hudson Bay people established themselves at Fort Yukon in 1847. In 1842 Mr. J. Bell, in charge of the Hudson Bay Post on the Peel River, which runs into the MacKenzie, from beyond the divide from the head waters of the Porcupine, crossed over and went down the Porcupine a way. In 1846 he followed it to its mouth, and saw the Yukon. In the following year Mr. A. H. Murray built Fort Yukon, and set up business. Well, it was here that the Archdeacon started to tell the savages of the Great Spirit—and they were mighty interested.

"The savages had some sort of a tradition that a certain canyon, which opened into the Yukon a short distance up stream from the Fort, was the home of bad spirits; they could hear them groaning, and they asked the missionary to 'put them wise.'[3] So when a bunch[4] arrived, one day in July 1863, he trotted the whole outfit off to the canyon.

[3] Inform them.

[4] Bunch—Party.

"Of course the missionary found the noises were caused by the wind or nothing, but, as the Siwashes said there were noises up the Creek, he said it was the wind.

"Walking along the shore, the Archdeacon saw a bit of something shining in the gravel and picked it up. It was a flake of gold sticking to a piece of mica, of which there's lots in the Klondike country—mica schist the scientists call it. So this was the first find of gold by a white man; but the Company was not looking for gold-hunters in their country, so the discovery was never followed up.

"The Siwash is A1 at asking questions—just about as bad as a six-year-old kid; and if a medicine man comes among them it is surprising what sort of conundrums they will bring him."

In this way John Berwick and his old-time mining-mate pleasantly passed the hours listening to the conversation of Spencer, by whom they were attracted.

On the third evening, at dinner—the three being seated together—they noticed some movement beginning amongst those of the company who were seated near the companion-way. Several were seen to rise and hurry away. Quickly the excitement spread, the saloon was soon empty of most of its feasters.

"Keep your seats, fellows; it's only some chechacho got the toothache," said Hugh. Shouts were heard, with a trampling and rush of feet on the upper deck. "The only thing that could happen—outside of fire—would be to run ashore or hit an iceberg. We are hardly far enough north for the icebergs yet—besides, if we had hit one, or run ashore, we should know it. If we caught fire, it would not be far to the shore anywhere along this route; and it is always well not to get stampeded in any case."

After dinner the friends entered the main saloon, and found groups of men talking excitedly, with others returning from the upper deck where the life-boats were stored. To the upper deck they went, and there they found Mr. Muggsley.

"I tell you, gentlemen, no officer or anybody else is going to keep me from the life-boats when a ship is sinking. I don't care for anybody! You stand by and let the officers and sailors run things—and they will fill the boats with women and their own friends—and look out for themselves. But I look out for John Muggsley! Big John Muggsley the boys call me! And it's a case like this that makes me glad I'm big and strong."

An excitable coal-heaver had found a stream of water entering by a sea-cock, which had been left open through carelessness; and, running up through the saloon to the boats, had started the excitement. Such trivial circumstances often cause most disastrous panics; and likewise tell tales of how certain men are made!

The ship eventually—after blinding snowstorms—entered Gastineau Channel. To the left was the great line of stamp mills pounding out the wealth of the mighty Treadwell quartz deposits on Douglas Island; to the right was the pioneer town of Juneau, with its gambling-halls and saloons enjoying the licence of the Alaska mining-camp.

The next stop for the ship was Skagway, where the sea journey would end on the morrow. The passengers were alert and astir. From then on it was to be a struggle.

CHAPTER IV
SOCIETY IN ALASKA

The weather had changed during the night; and as the two friends stepped on deck the following morning a chill and cutting wind met them from the north. Away above them towered the mountains, their peaks dazzling white against the sky. Behind them, to the south, was the Lynn Canal, walled with mountains. Before them were mountains, and yet more mountains. The cluster of tents and hastily constructed buildings, resting on a few square miles of gravel flats—comprising the town of Skagway—were robbed of any importance by the great uplifting walls of rock.

As they stood a voice hailed them. "Is this Skagway?" It was Mr. Muggsley who spoke.

"I fancy so," said John; "better ask the purser—here he comes."

"Do we have to climb those mountains to get to the Klondike?"

"Yes."

"But where is the White Pass?"

"There." The purser pointed to the mouth of a valley, which soon appeared blocked by a mighty mountain.

"And that is the White Pass?"

"It is."

"Say, purser, is that berth I had taken for the trip down again? If not, save it for me. I guess I'm wanted back in I-dee-ho."

Mr. Muggsley, the big man, the strong man, "Big Jack," as his friends called him, was suddenly possessed of "cold feet." The great uplifting mountains with their glittering peaks flung to heaven had quickened the cowardice of his craven soul.

Berwick and his comrade struggled ashore through the rushing freight-handlers and piled-up supplies. The freight which came from the Canadian port, Vancouver, had to be passed by the United States Customs, and the officers seemed few. There was a method of overcoming the Customs—by employing a "convoy," an official of the United States Customs, to escort the goods across the narrow strip into Canadian territory again. John made inquiries, and addressed a fellow in a wild garb, bespeaking a resident.

"Pay the duty, partner! These escort fellows are a bunch of grafters! They ain't no credit to the United States, I can tell you. Yes, pay duty, and hand an officer a ten-dollar bill on the side, or they'll keep you here a week, you bet!"

John decided to pay the duty. The convoy would cost $5.00 per day and expenses. He made an effort to get his goods passed, but without success— till he paid the ten-dollar bribe. George did the same. John did not like bribery; but—what else could he do?

It was afternoon ere they got through; and as they gained the town, a rough board-building with a great white cloth sign painted on it— "Restaurant, meals 50 cents"—met their gaze from the head of the wharf. Other buildings of similar character composed generally this section of the town, so they walked into the first.

It was a box of a place, as unfinished internally as externally. A dozen or so men, perched on high stools, were leaning against a board counter covered with white oilcloth. Behind the counter stood a woman and a girl; a range, where the chef was operating, at their back. A board partition divided off a sleeping apartment. The curtain that gave the room privacy was but half drawn. Articles of clothing, trunks, and boxes were strewn in disorder on the floor.

"Soup?" queried the lady as they took their seats. The cook filled two flat tin plates with a watery solution of tomatoes and rice. This they attacked. When the soup was finished two other tin plates were handed them, laden with cubical chunks of beef and gravy. Dishes of potatoes and boiled beans, with bread and butter in tin bowls, were lined upon the counter for each man to help himself from. At the end of the second course a plate, bearing a quarter section of sickly-looking apple-pie, was slid over to each.

The old lady presiding wore the smile of prosperity, and looked communicative, so John opened conversation. "Been in Skagway long?"

"Just a month."

"Doing well?"

"Sure thing! feed about three hundred people a day. Don't care if the rush never lets up."

"You've got a gold-mine here without the trouble of going to Dawson."

"Sure!—that is if Soapy don't put the whole town out of business. He makes the saloons and gambling-halls pay him royalty now, besides running shows himself; and I guess he'll be after us soon to make us anti-up too."

"I thought Alaska was a prohibition territory, no whisky sold here."

"Yes, that's what they say back East; but when you get up town you'll find every second place a saloon with all the hootch you want to drink, or have money to pay for."

"But how do they get the whisky?"

"Oh, that's easy enough. The hootch is consigned through to the Canadian side in bond; but when it is landed here they drill a hole in the barrel and take out the whisky. They refill the barrel with water, and it is packed over the summit."

"But it costs thirty cents a pound to put the water over the summit!"

"That don't matter—with whisky fifty cents a glass over the bar."

"Don't the officers know this is going on?"

"Sure thing they do; but they 'stand in. There is no graft like a whisky graft."

"Stand in" and "graft"!—the two Australians felt they knew the meaning of the terms, but they had yet to grasp how deep the meaning of "standing in" and "grafting," as understood by officialdom in Alaska and the Yukon, could be.

Berwick and his friend ate their pie, and departed to see the sights.

The main street of the town ran due north and south, and was lined with tents and buildings, finished and under construction. The street was devoid of snow, except in patches here and there; the ever-persistent wind from the north having generally swept the gravel clean. Sleighs, drawn by dogs or horses, passed smoothly over the ice, but shrieked in protest against the stone. Dogs and horses seemed everywhere in that rush of fifty thousand men. No man could enter the Yukon without a year's provisions, which meant that he must transport at least a thousand pounds in every case.

Along the streets vehicles were waiting to transport vast stores of supplies to White Pass City, twelve miles distant; after which dog-teams alone, or pack-animals, or the labour of the human animal, were necessary. Some pack-horses, mules, and burroes were passing down the streets to their stables, after having carried up their loads.

Men in outlandish garb were walking about; many wore what appeared to be night-shirts coming down to their knees, with hoods attached, and rings of fur around the wrists and the face of the hood. Some of the peculiar garments were made of blue drill, others even of bed-ticking, showing its dingy stripes. This garment was the parka.

Berwick and Bruce entered the Pack-Train Saloon and Gambling-hall, and met there the leaders of Alaska society: men and women of diverse morals and immoralities. In the great grab-bag system of the goldfields every man has an equal chance; and on the frontier custom affords but one field of diversion, which each may enjoy to the full extent of his purse and inclination. As muscle and endurance alone give eminence on the trail, so only money and extravagance command attention in the bar-room and at the gaming-table; and it is there that the illiterate squander their money over the bars and tables, finding pleasure in the open-mouthed admiration of the yokel as well as in the stimulation of the liquor or the excitement of the play.

At the bar of the Pack-Train stood a row of men, in widest diversity of costume, talking together and to women numbered among the fallen. Behind the bar were the roulette-wheel, the faro, the Black Jack tables, and the crap game. A large percentage of these men were actively engaged in putting supplies over the Passes, and were now squandering at the tables the money received in payment of that work. The thought struck John that probably not a man of them, wasting his money there, but had some one dependent to whom that money would be as a gift from heaven. Alas, for the recklessness of frontier life, where it so often happens that men regard a show of contempt for money as tantamount to personal eminence! Such scenes were not new to him. On the plains in his apprenticeship he had seen a cowboy shoot his revolver through a bar mirror—and cheerfully pay the exorbitant recompense demanded by the proprietor: and in Sydney he had watched a drunken sailor place a five-pound note between two slices of bread—and eat it!

Such scenes as this in the mushroom Alaska town may be ever-interesting to the students of human nature; they are also intensely pitiable, as Berwick found. What sight is sadder than that which shows man degraded, or woman fallen? Man, the noblest being in all creation; upbuilt, evolved through the ages; practically perfect in his parts: his body complex yet true; delicate and confident, enriched with a mind capable of holding dominion; and conscious of the inspiration of his Creator. To see him, mind and body, lost to dissipation, drawn from hope, truth, and love, fallen into the mire, is truly sadder than death.

From the Pack-Train Saloon the two friends visited several shops, and, notwithstanding the crowds therein, succeeded in adding to their supplies such necessities as were recommended by Hugh Spencer. Their purchases completed, they turned before the wind and went back to the restaurant. The air had taken on a greater chill; the mountain peaks shone with sunset gold.

CHAPTER V
SOAPY'S LITTLE GAME

"Soapy" Smith was a criminal, with a long record of robbery and murder. In early life he had been a common "faker" and sold soap, hence his sobriquet. His process consisted of wrapping small bits of laundry soap in paper, and including—or appearing to include—with several of the pieces a bank bill of varying value. Then he would mix all the pieces together, and picking a handful out of the mass, auction them. Needless to say every successful purchaser was a confederate!

In the Mining Camps of the Western States he later took more radical methods, making many enemies and some friends. When he and his gang wished to exterminate an enemy they would hunt him out in some saloon, gather about him, and play at fighting among themselves. Revolvers would be drawn and shots fired—the man "wanted" would be killed. It would be somewhat hard to find the actual man who fired the fatal shot, and, in any case, a subservient jury would bring in a verdict of "accidental" death.

The community that grew at the head of the Lynn Canal in the spring of 1898 was a complete hotbed for crime. There Soapy Smith established himself, and law and justice ceased to exist. Gold-seekers were enticed into games, and fleeced or openly robbed in the streets. Every saloon was owned by the desperado, or paid him tribute, and he drew revenue from every gambling-table.

Soapy Smith was the boss of these evil conditions. He was styled "Colonel," and spoken of as a candidate for Congress. A body of United States Regulars were stationed at Skagway, but did nothing. The Deputy United States Marshal would make promises, but take no action.

The second evening after the arrival of our party in Skagway the sky was overcast, and through the night a storm arose. So they stayed within doors all the next day; but towards night inaction told on them, likewise lack of fresh air. They became restless after their evening meal, and George finally said: "Let us go out"—and they went. George did not say where—nor did John ask. There was only one place to go to, and that was a saloon and gambling-hall: one was much the same as the other. Every saloon was a gambling-hall: every gambling-hall a saloon.

On the next night, in the vicinity of Skagway's Sixth Avenue, they wandered into a saloon which had no sign: the question of what its name was did not cross their minds! The air was foul, and floor space not too plentiful. Women stared at them, and "Passed them up." Not so the men. They moved on to the gaming-tables. John threw a coin on to the Black Jack table. To his surprise he won. He speculated again: again he won. Then he remembered the old dodge of letting the novice win a bit at first, so he decided he would keep on until he found himself losing. When he had won twenty dollars he put the money into his pocket, and went on with George to watch a man playing for heavy stakes at roulette. At this table there was never a word spoken, and the gold pieces passed from banker to player, from player to banker, without comment.

While the two were looking on they noticed a man come and stand by the banker, watch the game for a little while, glance shrewdly at them, and go away. Shortly afterwards another man did the same. John and George realised this attention, but said nothing. A third man came along, and bluntly asked them,

"Ever play roulette?"

"No; at least not often," said John.

"Good game."

"Yes."

"Ever shoot craps?"

"No."

"There's a table down at the end of the hall. Care to see it?"

They followed their entertainer to the dimly-lighted rear, where several men were leaning over a table throwing dice. They watched the game a bit, and found it uninteresting. They turned to go, when their new acquaintance made a move to follow—and asked in a hesitating way, "Have a drink?"

George declined.

The fellow pondered a bit, and then said in an ingratiating way, "Would you fellows like to see a big mountain goat I bought from the Siwashes to-day?"

John and George followed the man through a doorway into a cold room where a few candles were burning on a rough table. On the floor lay an immense mountain goat.

"My word!" said George, "what a beauty!"

They stood for some minutes surveying the dead monarch of the mountain crests, their entertainer taking one of the candles and holding it at the animal's head. Suddenly they heard groans, which appeared to come through the doorway at the opposite end of the room.

"What's that?"

The man took a candle and walked to the door, bending his head, as if listening intently. The groans were continued. John and George went over to him. He held the candle in his left hand, and appeared to haul at the door with his right. "Oh! Oh!" came from the room in tones of deepest distress. The fellow handed the candle to John, and then, catching the door with both hands, gave it a mighty wrench. The heavy plank door opened and showed a dark cavity, which drank up the slender light of the candle so effectually that they could distinguish nothing. Cautiously John entered, followed by George. The door was slammed; they were trapped.

"We're caught! Soapy has us," exclaimed George.

John turned, shaded the candle with his hand, and explored the room. It was not large, and it took him but a minute to make a circuit of the four walls.

"We're caught!" was said again.

"But there is no one here: where did the groans come from?" asked John.

"Don't know, if they weren't ventriloquism," replied George.

That seemed likely. John ran and gave the door a kick: it was solid as a wall.

"What will they do with us?" he asked.

"Freeze us to death; we'll freeze quick enough in this atmosphere."

The place was cold, clammy, benumbing. The walls were log; the floor of earth, sparkling with frost crystals; the roof was built of poles. There was no window. Here and there, where the crevices of the logs had not been thoroughly filled, and the air came in, there were patches of frost. They searched for some implement. The room was thoroughly bare—there was not even a billet of wood, let alone an axe, or saw. Things were at a pass. They were both to perish in horrible death. The cold was seizing them. They stamped up and down the room, and shouted. There was, there could be, no answer.

Frenzy came over them. Trapped! To perish of bitter cold! Horrible!... Horrible! To famish as caged animals. They saw their little destiny—to walk, and walk, and walk, and then to lie down and sleep till death, the reality, came. Their impotency galled them. How weak were their arms and strength against these walls of logs!

They marched about for an hour or more, encouraging each other as brave men will.

Then cries were heard faintly from the outside, and new noises, which grew, and continued to grow. A great blow shook the wall, and then another. John shouted; George shouted; the blows were repeated; then they heard voices and shouted again. The door was burst open and in rushed a number of men.

"Come, fellows, out of this, or you'll be cooked!"

It was the voice of Hugh.

They eagerly followed him through the room where the goat was, and out through a side door into the open, where a great glare met them. An outhouse was on fire. Men were rushing about and shouting; but Hugh kept on through the crowd, and the rescued followed him till they reached the safety of the street.

"Now we'd better duck for home," said Spencer. "I go with you"; and through the storm they struggled till they reached the Frau's restaurant.

She had not yet retired, so they called for supper—tea, bacon, and beans. After they had settled down Hugh told his story.

"You see, fellows, after I landed I went over to the Chilkoot to have a look at things there; but after talking to the fellows I reckoned that the White Pass was best for me, so back I comes. I was in the hall to-night with you fellows, but you did not see me; and I thought I would just lay back and see if you would hit the games. Then I kind of got a notion Soapy's men were watching you; so I thought I would watch the whole outfit. I see you go back to the crap-game, and then I see you go into the room with your bunco man—and then I don't see you come out; so I said to myself, you are there for keeps! Now there was with me one fellow I could rely on, so I asked him to keep an eye on that door, and I got out on the street to size up the building. I see towards the rear the wing you went into, so I walks down there, sizing things up. Round on the back side I see a door and a window, but the door had the snow piled up against it—besides, I knew they would not lock you in a room with a window in it, as you could easily kick that out.

"Then I looks at the walls, and I see by the end of the logs sticking out that there was a room which had neither window nor door to the outside, and I said, 'That's the cage!' So I ran back to the saloon and asked my friend there if anybody had come out, and he said 'No.' I came to the conclusion that I would make a bluff of going in at the door you came out of. It was no good; a fellow stopped me and said, 'This room is private.' This made me sure you were still there, so I commenced figuring out how I could get you free, and I thought hard. The thing was to get a crowd together; and as a dog fight is no good in Skagway in the middle of the night—especially in a snowstorm—I said to myself, 'Fire!' I remembered a building I took for a wood-shed lying near your skookum house,[5] so I just hunted it up, and after finding there was a lot of wood in it, with some hay, I set a match to it, and got out, taking an axe with me. In five minutes it was going fine, and I yelled 'Fire! fire! fire!' Then it was all easy. I struck the logs with the axe, and yelled there was somebody in there who would get burned; I busted in the door to the outer room, and then the one into where you were locked up—the other fellows following. I don't know what the other fellows around the fire will think you were doing in there; but I guess they won't ask any questions. Fellows don't ask questions in Soapy's town; it doesn't do them much good if they do."

[5] "Skookum House": Chinook Indian term for prison— literally "strong" house.

John and George expressed their gratitude very simply.

"I am going in over the White Pass," he continued, "and I figure, as us fellows can't keep clear of each other, that we'd better join forces."

"Done!" cried George.

"A good idea!" said John.

So it was agreed.

In the morning details were talked over, and business was arranged. Additional purchases were made, including two more dogs, thereupon named Tom and Jerry. Hugh induced his friends to part with much of their bedding, saying he had a large lynx-skin robe that was warmer than a dozen pairs of blankets, under which the three might sleep. A waterproof, a large tanned moose-skin, and a couple of pairs of blankets would be sufficient to lie upon. Then the commissariat was considered. Sugar, tea, evaporated potatoes, dried fruit, etc., to be used in the preparation of every meal, were put into small canvas bags, and those into a large sack. The general stores were put away in waterproof canvas sacks, which were marked to indicate contents. The axes of the party were ground and sharpened. At last all was ready for the advance.

CHAPTER VI
HITTING THE TRAIL

To be early on the trail was an essential to Hugh Spencer. He was up at four on the morning of the start, harnessed the dogs, carried the outfit to the sleigh, and lashed it on. Then he aroused his friends, who, when dressed, found that an early breakfast had been arranged for them of bacon, eggs, and beans.

"Better put lots next your ribs, for there isn't room to cook a meal on the trail between here and White Pass City," was the advice they received.

They left the restaurant, after a kindly good-bye from the old lady. John and George tied their hand-bags, containing underclothing, towel, soap, etc., and socks to the load. The main portion of their extra clothing was left in the general supplies.

Of the five dogs he of the stub tail—Dude the leader—was the only one that appeared to take an interest in the proceedings, for he was standing watching his master. The others were mere balls of fur lying in the snow. Hugh went ahead and harnessed himself in the cord that was tied to the front of the sleigh, and grasped the "gee-pole," lashed as a single shaft on the right side of the sleigh.

"Mush," he ordered. Dude gave a tug at the traces, and the other dogs stood up.

"Mush," was ordered again. The whole five dogs strained at the traces, in a half-hearted sort of way, not sufficient to move the load. Hugh then let go his hold of the pole, threw off his harness, and picked up a whip that was tucked under the lashings of the load. Behind Dude was Two Bits; then came Four Bits, Tom and Jerry. Beginning with Two Bits, he gave each a cut with the whip, causing heart-rending howls; but Dude stood throughout the ordeal, evidently oblivious to the sufferings of his companions; his tongue protruding. He was a picture of conscious virtue. Dude knew these signs of the trail, the stern, hard life, the cut of the whip, the cry of the dog.

Hugh then cracked the whip, re-harnessed himself in the cord, and grasped the gee-pole.

"Mush," he ordered. The five dogs strained at the traces, taking quick, furtive glances over their shoulders at the man with the whip. The load moved; the march towards the great and golden Klondike had started.

Early as they were they saw, as they reached the main street, others on the trail; and up the long avenue heading north between the great mountains horse-teams, dog-teams, and men unaided were drawing their loads. The wind was roaring down the pass, cutting their faces like a knife. They now appreciated the special virtues of the parka, for with hood drawn over their head, as they bent before the gale, their faces largely escaped the cutting blasts; and the light material of which the garment was made was wonderfully effective in keeping the wind from their bodies.

Although the recent storm had improved the travelling, it was not long before the sleigh grated on gravel and stopped, the dogs appearing instinctively to realize that the noise meant further effort was useless. Hugh said nothing, but disengaged himself from his harness, went to the rear of the load, and undid a coil of rope from either side, to which Berwick and Bruce were harnessed also. He then resumed his position. "Mush!" The three men and five dogs threw themselves against the load. There was a shriek from the gravel, and the sleigh glided again over the soft snow.

The difficulty being over, Hugh told his friends to disengage themselves and throw the cords back on the load, which they did, after protesting that they had better remain in harness and help to pull.

"No, you fellows can each take a turn at the gee-pole when I get tired," Hugh said.

The dogs would stop for any excuse; it was only necessary for Hugh to pass the time of day with a south-bound traveller, when the train would stand, their tongues lolling out, their eyes vacantly staring. 'Tis the nature of the beast. The native dogs of the north never give the impression that they work because they feel it their duty. They work because they know there is a stronger will than theirs behind them, a will with a whip.

The party moved steadily along for a mile or two, when the road left the flats and took to the side hill at the right hand of the canyon. A considerable amount of work had been done, and the trail was in good shape; but they had not gone far before they were met by a toll-gate.

"Twenty-five cents each, and two dollars and a half for the dog-team," was demanded of them, which they paid. The keeper of the toll-gate seemed happy; he was prospering, and those who employed him were making money. John and George thought the charge excessive, but Hugh was exercising his wits, calculating how much the proprietors made out of what he called their "graft."

Not far beyond the toll-gate they met an old man sitting by a fire under the lee of a wall of rock. He was off the trail in a sort of little cove, and on the much-betramped snow around was a sleigh, and by it five goats in harness. The old man merely looked up as the three friends approached, and went on poking the fire.

"Well, partner, enjoying the scenery?" asked Hugh, in his good-natured manner.

"No—I wish I was dead."

"How's that?"

"These ornery goats here, I can't do nothing with them, an' if it wasn't for poor little Bess, back home, I'd shoot them and meself too."

"What's the trouble?"

"Well, the ornery critters won't pull a pound, and the fellow who sold them to me down in Seattle said they was just the thing for the Pass— better'n dogs, for I could feed them on birch browse; but I lit out from Skagtown[6] four days ago and could get no further than this. I pretty near had to pull sleigh and goats too to get this far; and I pitched camp here, where I've stayed ever since. You see it's this way—the old woman died last fall, and after she died the poor old farm went plumb to pieces, hard times, and mortgage falling due; so I got a sickening of the old place without the old woman, and I let the farm go and put little Bess to school for a year, and lit out for the Klondike. Bess ain't Bess by rights; she was christianized Matilda Jane, and we called her Bess for short. Well, the old woman was always building on bringing up Bess a real lady, and afore she died I promised I'd give Bess a good schooling and help all I could, and I took to the Klondike, hearing all a fellow had to do was to get there, and he'd be rich. Here I am now, and I ain't got no more money. I'm just trying to make up my mind to shoot the blamed goats and pull my stuff back to Skagtown and sell it. Then I guess I'll go packing on the Chilkoot along with the Siwashes."

[6] Skagway

The old man seemed to forget the presence of the strangers, and muttered, "Poor little Bess! Poor little Bess! I was hoping to make her a real lady with silks, an' satins, an' diamonds, an' kid gloves, an' fancy eyeglasses."

Hugh cracked the whip, John tightened on the cord, the dogs threw themselves into the traces; and the trio was on its way up the Pass. No one spoke for some time; each was thinking of the old man's tale, and of such as that old man there were hundreds in the Passes.

The trail, as they struggled along, proved to be more and more built against the side hill, and frequently the sleigh showed a disposition to slide into the canyon, so that all were compelled to give attention to it. But the three men taking turn at the gee-pole, they had soon crossed Kill-a-man Creek, and were at the foot of Porcupine Hill. The time had passed quickly, and the air, though cold, was highly stimulating. George and John voted the parka a wonderful garment.

Arriving at the base of the hill, Hugh quickly undid the fastenings, piled half the load on the side of the trail, and relashed the balance to the sleigh; then he and John set about the task of taking the first load to the top of the hill, while George mounted guard at the base. Hugh took the gee-pole, John harnessed himself in the cord that was attached to the left-hand rear of the sleigh; so they set out.

The hill made a rise of several hundred feet in the first quarter of a mile, and in some places seemed almost standing on end; but straining, pulling, tugging, men and dogs both, they eventually reached the top. They soon had the sleigh unloaded, and Hugh was off down again for the remainder of the load. In three-quarters of an hour they were all together again. Then began the descent, which was almost as acute as the rise had been. They adjusted the necessary brakes by tying a piece of rope around each runner.

Before leaving the summit of Porcupine Hill they had a good look at the view. Across the valley in front, set in a basin of the mountains, was a collection of buildings and tents, constituting White Pass City. Two long lines of men and teams marked the White Pass, one on the left side of the canyon, the other on the canyon bottom. The hillside trail was used by horses, mules, and oxen, while in the wedge-like canyon bottom men and dogs toiled. The reason for the hillside trail was that its ascent was more gradual, the lower trail having many abrupt rises up which horses and oxen could not clamber.

The scene of toil and labour, backed by the sublimity of the surroundings, impressed the beholders; but the party came to life again with Hugh's order, "Mush!"

The dogs struggled with the load over the brink of the decline down which the sleigh quickly passed, and the party was not long in reaching White Pass City. This was the first depot out from Skagway, and was distant there-from twelve miles. From White Pass City to Lake Bennett the distance was twenty-four miles, so they were now one-third of the way. But the twelve miles they had passed was the easiest part of the journey.

Saloons and restaurants in wide array, and numerous stables in the shape of tents tied down and guyed against the ever-recurring blasts, comprised White Pass City. And how the wind did blow from the funnel-shaped canyon across the basin in which the town was built!

Notwithstanding the cold, beasts of burden were standing in all directions, tied to posts and rails, while the dogs seemed without number. It being now late in the day, there were more teams returning from the summit and Bennett than were setting out. Amongst those returning they met a man with a dozen pack-mules. Long icicles hung from his moustache, powdery snow was driven into the folds of his parka, his cheeks were alternate patches of blue and crimson. His manner was blustering, because he was glad at having returned, and proud that he had done so without losing any horses.

"Hello," said Hugh, "what's it like on the summit?"

"What's it like! Look here, stranger, if I owned hell and that summit, I'd sell the summit and live in hell, so help me! What's the matter with the summit? Why, if that cursed wind ain't blowing from the north cold enough to freeze hell, then it's blowing from the south and snowing as if all the feather beds in the New Jerusalem were being split open and shaken loose. I'll be hanged if the Mounted Police ain't got a stable and store-house scooped out under the snow, and the roof standing up like as if it was a rock. About sixty feet of snow has fallen up there this winter; and how them poor devils of policemen hold things down in tents is more than I know. A fellow can tackle it for a day or two, but these fellows have been up there since early in February!"

"It's a way they have in the Army," suggested George, always an ardent Briton.

"Those fellows are different from any Army fellows I ever seed," was the stranger's reply.

The pack-train was called to a halt. The communicative stranger and his assistants were taking the saddles off the mules; but for once the dogs were impatient and restless: instinct told them they were near the end of their day's work and the prospect of food. So Hugh let them have their way, and they drew up in front of a restaurant which bore the legend, "Meals, seventy-five cents."

"Better go in and eat, fellows, and I'll look after the dogs," said Hugh.

His friends demurred, but he insisted; so they entered the restaurant.

There was the same motley crowd feeding in the same savage manner as at Skagway. Everybody smoked on the trail—in all places and under any condition—save where the pipe froze and refused its duty.

The hour was between two and three. Berwick and his comrade thought they had never been so hungry. How they relished the hot soup, and the meat, potatoes, and beans! And when they drank ...! George finished his dinner first, and scrambled off to relieve Hugh, whom he found cutting up pieces of raw meat for the dogs.

"Raw meat ain't any too good for dogs, but after they get over the summit they will get down to boiled rice and tallow — and that ain't far off."

Hugh was certainly the favourite of the dogs just then, but soon after George's arrival he put the piece of meat he had been dividing into a sack and threw it on the sleigh, and hurried to the restaurant, saying that he would boil the rest of the meat for the dogs after he himself had something to eat. "Look out for Soapy's gang" was his final warning to George.

After Hugh had his dinner (dinner is the mid-day, supper the evening, meal on the trail) he remarked that he would take a mooch round. When he returned he greeted his friends with:

"Say, I found a fellow I know here running one of these stables, and he has a tent with a lot of hay in it, and says we can sleep in that, which will save us making camp. We can put the dogs inside and run less chances of having them stolen; also the grub."

So Dude was aroused from his sleep; four other doggy noses were withdrawn from under four bushy tails, and to the accompaniment of howls the load was removed to the hay-tent, the dogs unharnessed, the load unpacked. Hugh undid the bedding and spread it on a pile of straw.

"This will be the last bed we'll strike for some time after we leave here," was his remark.

He grabbed the sack with the meat, and went off to see if he could find space on a stove to boil it. He soon returned with the meat, as well as a bucket in which were canine dainties — kitchen scraps.

"Chuck it into you," was Hugh's remark to the dogs as he threw them the food; "you'll have to work to-morrow."

As there was nothing to do now till that morrow, the three again strolled out to look at the trail, up which the full flow of traffic was now toiling. Profanity filled the air. The travellers cursed the trail; they cursed their horses, cursed their dogs, the wind, the country generally.

They wandered into a saloon, which, as ever, was reeking with tobacco, and vibrating to the notes of "Home, sweet Home," reeled off on a gramophone. Hugh looked cautiously at the company. "Soapy's men!" he whispered; so he and his companions went. John noticed that a good deal of money was being won at the tables; but Hugh told him that the men who were winning were Soapy's staff.

"They seem to run a wonderful system," said John.

"Yes; Soapy pretty nearly owns the whole shop from the Lynn Canal to the summit."

"But why does he stop at the summit?"

"Police."

"But they have police on this side."

"Not the same."

"How do you account for that?"

"Don't know: discipline! The Canadian police are not grafting. Fellows I've met from the inside tell me that Cap Constantine gave records for all the rich claims in Bonanza, and neither he nor any of the rest of the Mounted Police grafted any. That's what I call honest; but now, since the records have been taken away from the police, there's nothing but grafting going on. Fellows have to give up half interest in claims to the officials before they can get record; and even the Government is grafting officially with this ten per cent. royalty. If some of those Members of Parliament back in Canada were here, with this proposition, getting over these Passes, they'd think they had a right to all they'd found in this country. And now they are taking part of it away—it's a shame, I call it."

They had walked up the lower trail leading to the summit. Whatever men and horses were to be seen were making down the Pass, for the trail that clung to the side of the mountain was so narrow that two horses, going in opposite directions, could not pass each other; so in the morning the horses passed up the trail, and in the afternoon down. That was the unwritten law. They returned to the sleeping quarters.

Every dog, except Dude, had his nose under his tail, and was apparently oblivious to all outside concerns. Dude's tail was not long enough to cover his nose, and Hugh noticed his eyes quiver and open slightly. On the floor was the empty meat sack. The five dogs had demolished the large piece of dead horse.

"That's Dude," said Hugh.

"Which?" asked John.

"Why, stealing that meat. Before we get to Dawson you'll know what a high-class article in the stealing line he is. However, there'll be lots more dead horses: they kill about a dozen a day between here and Bennett."

"How do they manage that?"

"Wait till to-morrow, and you'll see."

CHAPTER VII
HUGH'S PHILOSOPHY

The stars were still shining when the friends tore themselves, stiff and sore, from under their lynx-skin robe on the morrow to dress in the chill atmosphere of the tent; but the sounds of movement were everywhere. Commands, embellished with profanity, were being shouted. When the three adventurers, after a hurried breakfast, eagerly went out a sickly light was spreading over the mountains, which seemed spectral and immense.

"We'll take the flour, sugar, and hardware in the first two loads," remarked Hugh, as he began selecting these supplies; "and it won't do any harm to hang our bacon sack from a rafter while we are away, as a stray malamoot might get in here. These blamed dogs will chew a tin can open to get at the meat inside."

The plan of campaign suggested by Hugh and endorsed by the others was to divide the supplies in three loads; to take two, comprising the reserve stores, to the summit and cache them; then, on the following day, to carry the remainder of the stuff right through to Log Cabin, or to Bennett if they could manage it, and establish a camp there. This depended on the condition of the trail.

Early as they were, there were scores of outfits setting out, and many were ahead of them.

They had not gone far when they met two men and a dog-team; one of the men was belabouring the dogs with a whip, making them howl dreadfully. Dude and the rest of the team halted, and, with their masters, watched the proceedings. The dogs belaboured were soon tangled among the traces in fine confusion. Each animal, as he saw a stroke coming his way, jumped sideways with a howl and buried his nose and feet in the snow. The cruelty aroused the anger of John and George, who made a move towards the brute with the whip. Hugh caught him by the arm and pulled him back.

"Better not make yourself a Humane Society in this country; you'll only get into trouble—besides, he ain't hurting the dogs: wait!"

When the man rested from the belabouring, Hugh asked to be allowed to "try the dogs."

The fellow glared angrily at him; but then, with a surly nod, gave the permission. Hugh started with the leaders, and worked down the whole line, placing the dogs in order once again, hauling them about, but saying nothing. Then he took the gee-pole, and ordered "mush." The leader looked back over his shoulder, as did the dog next him. "Mush!" again cried Hugh. The dogs drew steadily at their collars, glancing furtively at their new master. Hugh once more encouraged them, and when the load began to move passed on his charge to the owner, who had the grace to look sheepish.

"To handle dogs," said Hugh, when he had rejoined his party and had resumed the trail, "you've got to get them frightened of you; and moving round them, silent-like, puts fear in their souls. You see, that fellow wasn't really hurting them; they could hardly feel that light whip through their fur, and their feet and noses, where they are tender, they stuck in the snow. As for howling—it comes natural to malamoots. No—you've got to treat them just as you do women."

The trail often became precipitous, but as the combined strength of the three men and the dogs was sufficient to lift the load bodily, their difficulties were well overcome.

They had not been out of the White Pass City an hour when George shouted "Look!" and pointed to the mountain-side to the left. The trail away above them was lined with horses, moving slowly forward; but down the mountain-side eight burroes were plunging—head tied to tail as is the custom. Every dog team on the lower trail had stopped to watch the sight, for there was a great rattling of rock and a general shout calling attention to the catastrophe. The unfortunate creatures soon reached the base of the slide and were lost in the soft snow. They struggled, and they disappeared. One more sacrifice to that dreadful trail, which, during the Klondike rush, had claimed the lives of thirty-five hundred animals! In that canyon, between White Pass City and the summit, during the spring of 1898, it was possible to walk long distances on the bodies of dead horses, and to this day the line of march is marked by protruding bones, indicating the graves of the patient and faithful creatures, sacrificed to man's insatiable greed for gold.

"Now you see where the dog-food comes from," remarked Hugh.

The accident had occurred a little in front of them, and shortly afterwards two men were seen floundering through the soft snow down the side hill to the beaten trail, along which the dog-teams were pressing.

"You had hard luck," Hugh called to them.

"Yes, I couldn't keep that blame bell burro from experimenting how near he could go to the side without falling off, till at last he got his needings," replied one of the drivers.

"Whose outfit were they?"

"Rivers; and the Canadian Government owns the supplies—police stuff. They can stand it."

The two drivers went on down the trail to White Pass City.

The Canadian Government was evidently not popular. The iniquities of the royalty on gold, and the grafting current in the Gold Commissioner's office in Dawson were resented.

As the party progressed up the Pass, they found its walls coming closer together, making the canyon so narrow that the horse trail on the mountain-side appeared directly overhead. Numbers of dead cattle appeared by the side of the path, telling of the calamities of the trail. Veterans of the trail will tell weird tales of horses, goaded by whip and burden, deliberately throwing themselves into the canyon below—seeking surcease from suffering in death. As the canyon became narrower, so did the trail become more congested. It also grew steeper as they neared the summit, and men and dogs had frequently to pause for rest. It appeared to John a curious struggling mass that surrounded him, strange oaths in all accents came to his ears. The multitude were striving in a race in which brute force alone could conquer.

They came to a party in trouble, and overheard an argument.

"I tell you the territory clear through to Lake Bennett belongs to the United States, and I'm convoy for the United States Customs. I ain't going to let you get over the summit until you pay my wages for four days more, that is, two days from the summit to Lake Bennett loaded, and two days back again from Bennett to Skagway, travelling light, and that's going some too. It amounts to thirty-two dollars, at eight dollars per day—so all you've got to do is pay up."

"No, you don't own the land beyond the summit. Don't you see the English flag up there—that red thing flying from the tent pole? All you've got to do is show me over the summit, and we're quits. I've paid you forty dollars already: three days doing nothing at White Pass City during the storm; and you lost the money playing Black Jack. I ain't got any more money to pay you, anyway. I can't pay you when I ain't got the money."

"Well, dig for it; sell part of your outfit. You can't bluff me. I'm an officer of the United States Customs, and I'm on to my job."

"More grafting," muttered Hugh.

So it was that these convoys, armed with authority more or less real, harassed and blackmailed the victims.

They were now near the summit, in the midst of the last struggle which would put them over the most difficult portion of the trail, and the excitement was general. There was a deal of shouting, and a great renewal of effort. The horse trail and the lower trail merged into one.

At last they were through. The narrow defile curved to the right; an open basin appeared, with strewn tents and an endless promise of supplies; and—most conspicuous of all!—side by side the flags of Britain and the United States were flying.

A dozen members of the Canadian Mounted Police, wearing the uniform of England's Queen, were examining freight, with their backs to the wind, or passing in and out of a tent, half buried in snow, which served as an office. This was the second great depot out from Skagway, and piled about everywhere were loads of freight. Outfits stood about in disorder, awaiting the returning tide of men, while constantly teams were arriving from, or setting out to, Bennett.

The outfit of Hugh and his companions was finally passed by eleven o'clock. Goods of Canadian manufacture were allowed to pass free, and the charges against the few American goods were of no great amount. Hugh selected a projecting rock on which to make his cache, and the policeman who examined his baggage, and whose good offices the party had won, promised to keep an eye on their goods.

"Soapy doesn't operate on this side," said the man in uniform significantly.

"We could coast back in half an hour if the trail was clear," Hugh remarked, as they started on the return.

As it was, they sat on the sleigh most of the way to White Pass City, which they reached at noon—as a man was pounding a great triangle of steel with an iron rod, announcing dinner.

The three were very well pleased with their morning's work.

There were not quite so many teams on the trail in the afternoon, and they reached the summit by half-past three. The sun had been shining all day, so that the atmosphere seemed mellower; and the wind did not blow so strongly. After passing the goods they had time to climb the ridge on which the police tents were erected. From thence they gazed down the valley, which they knew was the uppermost watershed of the mighty Yukon, whose course makes a great curve of twenty-four hundred miles ere it flows into the Behring Sea. Far in the distance they could see a stunted growth of timber, but their immediate surroundings were mountains, hardly less overpowering than in White Pass City.

The view impressed them—the scene was weird in its desolation; they felt that stirring incidents were to take place in that great valley before them.

"Looks as if we would have a touch of spring to-morrow, and I guess we had better have our snow-glasses ready before we set out," said Hugh.

CHAPTER VIII
OVER THE SUMMIT

Hugh's prediction came true, for, on the morning following, a gentle breeze was blowing from the south, soft with the touch of spring. The first light that came over the mountains was a softening blue.

"Roll out and get the kinks out of you, fellows, we've got to be first on the trail to-day."

They had breakfast, the dogs were harnessed, and the party on the march by half-past four. Though the light was uncertain it was not hard to keep the trail. By six they were at the summit, greeting the police sentinel who had been on guard there through the night, and marvelling at the wealth of colours that lit the eastern sky.

"Mush!"

The dogs were off. The sleigh slid down upon the frozen plain of Summit Lake. The lightness with which it glided along seemed to assure the party that their troubles were over. As the dogs trotted along it required a pace faster than a walk to keep up with them; so Hugh induced his two companions to sit on the load, saying that he would take a ride after a while. At nine they reached Log Cabin—passed without a halt, it being merely a police depot used for cutting firewood, though it had been the Customs post before the Canadian Government had asserted proprietary rights to the summit. Almost invariably, when greetings were exchanged with those met on the trail, the humour played about Soapy.

"Say, you're hustling. I guess you ain't chechachoes. How's Soapy? going to run for President next trip?"

"I guess so, if he ain't hung in the meantime. Looks like that he was the whole thing in the Passes."

As the party at one o'clock drew into Bennett, they saw one party eating dinner in the open, with sleigh loaded and dogs harnessed beside them. A pile of spruce boughs denoted where these strangers had slept, and where their tent, now drawn up on their sleigh, had been erected.

"Moving camp?" asked Hugh.

"Yes."

"I don't suppose you're going to take your location away with you?"

"I guess not."

"Then it will just suit us, and we can use your fire. This is what I call lucky," said Hugh, as he began unlashing the load and throwing the bundles of supplies on the spruce bed.

George was busying himself undoing the supplies while John replenished the fire. George cooked bacon; Hugh mixed flour, baking-powder, and water for slap-jacks—the large pancakes of the frontier. As they worked Hugh re-opened conversation with the strangers.

"Where's your new location?"

"Down the lake, five miles. Got wind of a good bunch of timber there, and hauled a load down this morning. One of our fellows stayed down making camp while us two came back for the rest of the stuff."

"How long have you been coming from Skagway?"

"Three weeks—a week here, and two weeks getting over the Pass. Contracted with a fellow to put through our stuff at thirty cents a pound, but finally had to buy dogs and haul it ourselves. And then the storms have been something fearful up to the last few days: sort of Dakota blizzard every day almost, after which trails was mighty bad hauling. This sort of weather comes hard on a fellow who was reared in California."

"I guess it would come hard on a fellow reared at the North Pole! You fellows will have your boat built in lots of time."

"Yes, if we don't take to quarrelling like the rest of the blame fools around here."

"What are those fellows doing here?" Hugh nodded to the great array of tents spread over the sand hills that lie between Lake Bennett and Lake Lindeman.

"Most of them don't know what they are doing; but I guess they put in their time quarrelling. Old Moss-backs from the East, who have lived neighbours all their lives, and been best of friends, have come up here partners, and before they got through the Passes were calling each other the names they heard used by the old-timers to their dogs! It takes the police all their time settling disputes. The habit seems to have took all round, now that they are through their troubles and have only straight hard work, whip-sawing lumber, ahead of them. Why, say! I saw two fellows the other day dividing their outfit. They took a two-faced axe and drove it into a log, and with the face sticking up and a hammer they cut a whip-saw in two, making it no good for either, and swearing at each other all the time till you could smell sulphur. They cut stoves in two, and boats, after working hard to build them. It seems a new kind of bughouse that has got hold of them."

The strangers were now washing up their dishes and packing them away. "Here, take this, hand me a plate," and one of them poured some stewed prunes out of a pot, and from another emptied into a second plate beans and bacon.

"But you fellows could take these along!" protested Hugh.

"No, we couldn't; they'd get spilled; besides, we have some beef-steak for supper. Some fellows down near the lake killed an ox this morning, and you can get steak for six bits per pound—if it ain't all gone. Good-bye!"

The strangers went off down the hill to the lake.

Pipes were lit, and the three lay in the sun smoking. The day was glorious and the party had removed their snow-glasses, so that they were able to view their surroundings to the full. Mountains gleamed and glistened everywhere in the distance, but did not appear so overpowering or inspiring as in the Pass, though more beautiful. How pure the air seemed, and spotless the snow!

Though the sun was warm and the party comfortable, there were duties to be performed; so, not without groans, Hugh and his friends started to erect camp. After the tent was up, Hugh put pots of beans, prunes, and rice on to boil—the rice being for the dogs, as there was small prospect of getting dead horse in Bennett.

After the bed had been made and the supplies stored in the tent, and more wood cut, there was nothing to be done; so Hugh went off among the tents on a "mooch round"—with an eye for beef-steak! George, acting as cook, stayed at home.

John also went sight-seeing. He took a different trail from his friend, crossed to the west side of the stream that led from Lake Lindeman to Lake Bennett, and walked in the direction of a smoke stack, the local saw-mill, half a mile distant.

As he strolled through the array of tents, he heard angry voices proceeding from one of them.

"I tell you he's no good," one was shouting. "I had to pull most all the way up the Chilkoot—him saying he had rheumatism, backache, toothache, heartburn—everything but the mumps, for them I could see. An' then, when we did get over the summit, it's me who had to do all the pulling."

"It's a lie—you're a low dog; and didn't I have to take whisky along before you'd travel at all? I tell you, Mr. Policeman, he's no good, he's a skunk, and I wouldn't take a skunk into Dawson with me, not if I never got there, nor never saw the million dollar claim I guess I'm going to get—if ever I get there."

John, passing beside the tent, could see the two disputants each seated on a log of wood, with a red-coated policeman standing in front of them.

"Well," said the policeman, "if you fellows can't get on together, the only thing to do is split up the outfit and each take what belongs to him."

"I own the whole outfit," said the man with the many diseases.

"No, you don't; I own the tent, the stove, the sleigh, and a whole lot of the grub," shouted the other.

John passed on. Another petty problem for the Mounted Police! They are great men, great workers, those yellow-legs!

There were some industrious 'prentices at Lake Bennett, for down along the shore were numerous groups of men, building boats.

"Like beef-steak?" asked Hugh, as John returned.

"Yes—rather."

A big frying-pan, with sizzling meat, was busy on the little tin camp stove.

"Keep an eye on the meat, John, while I get some water."

Hugh took a pail and went off to the river.

George Bruce was away with an axe getting wood, so John was left in charge. Shortly afterwards George came along, hauling a log of firewood by an axe driven into it. John ran to assist him, and when the two had returned with the wood Hugh was arriving with the water. John again turned his attention to the frying-pan: the largest piece of steak was gone!

"What has happened to the steak?" John asked.

Hugh looked. A grim smile came over his face.

"Dude!"

"Dude could not steal steak out of a frying-pan?"

"Not Dude? You bet your life that's where the steak has gone to. And there is no use licking him; the only way to cure Dude of stealing is to cut his tail off behind his ears. I told you Dude would rather steal than eat: and this shows how careful you must be."

Dude was lying a picture of innocence on the snow. How he could maintain an appearance of unconcern with a broiling hot beef-steak inside him was a marvel! John looked at him amazed: the smallest slit of a black eye was watching him.

"I was only away about three minutes."

"Half a minute is enough for Dude. He likes beef-steak!"

Hugh refilled the pan and then—civilization knows no artifice to better the enjoyment of such a meal!

They were partakers, too, of another repast—their souls were fed by the glories of nature: the sun was setting; its splendour spread from high in the heavens to the rugged range that yesterday had resisted them. On that vast canvas were painted salmon-coloured clouds with long ribbons of yellow, bearing the lustre of burnished gold.

It was the extreme of grandeur, awe-inspiring and ennobling. The evening was very still.

CHAPTER IX
STORM AND STRESS

It was five o'clock on the morrow before the party was up, and six o'clock before, breakfast cooked and eaten, John and Hugh were on the road to the summit. They were to travel the twenty miles there, and return with one thousand pounds of supplies.

The glow of the sun was already upon the mountains when they set out.

"Say! it's going to be a hot day, and it's going to thaw some. It'll make hauling easy, but our feet will be pretty wet; good thing we've got some dry socks and rubbers in our outfit at the summit. Another thing is, we're going to meet a whole lot of fellows on the trail the way we're going to-day; and, what's worse, we'll get more of them coming back."

Sure enough, after they left Log Cabin, they could see the toilers coming, winding in a snake-like procession among the hills.

Hugh had prophesied correctly. By eleven o'clock they were in their shirt-sleeves. The dazzling whiteness of the snow, reflected from all sides, made the use of smoke-glasses necessary; but the perspiration, dimming the glass, troubled their sight. The end of John's nose became painful; his cheeks burned. It reminded him of the after-effects of his first sunny spring day on the water in England.

They met and passed scores of teams, and still more were pouring over the summit when they arrived there at one o'clock. It was half-past two before they had their feet encased in German socks and rubber shoes, and their load ready again for the trail.

"We can't make home before dark, but we should be able to make Log Cabin by seven, after which the trail will be clear, and we should arrive by ten. This trail will be mighty good going after it starts to freeze, which it will do, soon as the sun goes down."

At four o'clock they were three miles on the trail. There was already frost in the air.

Ere another half-hour had passed Hugh felt his cheek smitten by a gust of wind, laden with particles of ice.

"I thought so!" he exclaimed; "these last few days have shown too large a pay streak of spring to last. We're in for trouble. It will be down on us in half an hour. All we can do is to keep on as we are going, steadily. I guess we shall make Log Cabin, but not with this load. The soft snow makes a thousand pounds too much for the dogs. Look!" He pointed to a miniature cyclone coming along the trail, drinking up the ice particles as it whirled. It struck them sharply as a gust of wind.

The first contact of the storm was cold and cutting; then the wind veered, and down came the snow. The sleigh was soon too heavy.

"The only thing is to cache the sleigh and turn the dogs loose; the chances are we won't be able to keep the trail in this storm; and if we do come out alive, we won't be able to find the sleigh if we abandon it far from the trail."

"Do you think the storm will be very bad?"

"It's bad now, ain't it? How long will it be before there is eighteen inches of snow on this trail? For a time we can keep it by feeling it hard under us; but we are liable to get off it—and once lost, there is no finding it again. Mind, the wind is blowing from the right, half to the rear. Here's a tree; I've noticed this lone spruce before, and we can find it again. Let us stand the sleigh up against it, and turn the dogs loose."

So to the tree dogs and men struggled; the dogs were unhitched, harness was piled on top of the load. Then, with a great effort, the men managed to up-end the load against the tree.

Hugh called Dude to him, and pulled an old envelope out of his pocket, on which he scratched: "Cached sleigh on north side of trail by spruce tree, five miles from the summit.—Hugh Spencer." This he tied to a handkerchief, and that to Dude's collar.

"It's no harm letting George know where the grub is, for if we don't find camp again, Dude will."

The dogs went, Dude leading, and were soon lost to sight.

Down the trail the two men strode. The snow was six inches deep already, the wind piling it upon the trail. The weather did not feel cold; in fact, both were comfortably warm. For an hour they plodded along. Occasionally one would plunge into the soft snow and scramble back on to the beaten trail. Conversation was not much indulged in.

The light began to fail, yet they stumbled along. There was nothing they could recognize in the boulders and cliffs that loomed around them in a deathly monotony.

For half an hour darkness was upon them, when Hugh remarked that Log Cabin could not be far away. Immediately following his remark they plunged into soft snow. The trail seemed to have come to an end; but this could not be so. They retraced their steps and regained firm footing. They felt cautiously around with their feet, but could find the underlying snow hard only in the direction whence they came.

"I guess we're off the trail, and have walked along a bank where the wind has packed the old snow good and hard. Looks to me as if we was lost."

"Don't give up," said John.

"Give up! I ain't giving up; but we're lost. I won't give up as long as I can wiggle."

"What had we better do?"

"Keep moving! If you don't, you freeze!" Spencer's voice was low and serious as he said, "Keep the wind on your right side; and if you've got any last will and testament to make, scratch it on a piece of paper and leave it in your pocket before your hands get numb, or your mind weak. We're up against it hard! We will stay together, of course; but should we get separated, don't move too fast, or you will tire yourself out and go to sleep in the snow. Don't let sleep take hold of you, or you're dead! Just keep moving fast enough to keep warm, or, at least, from freezing; go down hill rather than up; and don't fall over a cliff. Have you ever been up against a life-and-death proposition? If not, you are pretty near one now."

They proceeded on their uncertain journey, but were soon floundering in soft snow. They kept on. It was easy enough to say "keep going down-hill," but, so far as John was concerned, he seemed to be walking up-hill all the time. They frequently exchanged shouts, and so remained together.

For hours they plodded on, the snowfall growing less, but the cold greater.

John began to act, to call, mechanically. His mind in that desolate trampling was transported to happier places. He thought of his Alice Peel. She was probably, he mused, thinking of him also. Did her mind ever picture such experiences as he was now realizing? She would possibly read in the newspapers of the great rush of gold-seekers over those terrible mountains and through the stormy passes. If he should die in that storm, and months afterwards she heard of his demise?... The thought drifted along to several loose ends. He must not sleep, or he would die; and it was his duty to live; but—oh! to sleep!... His father, and the old school, the church services! How much he would like to hear the old organ and the choir!... It had been the family wish that he should take Holy Orders, and he had refused the vocation, feeling it not his. Had he done right? He believed yes.... He might be about to meet his Creator. What might his record be?...

His mind went back to an occasion in Australia, when he had been lost in the Bush, and had wandered for days without water, till some blacks found him. He remembered, before going into unconsciousness with his back against a rock, that a vulture was watching him. He had taken a piece of stone, and, pretending it was a pistol, had pointed it at the bird....

John Berwick's mind was picturing sand and heat, while above him roared the Arctic storm.

How cold it was getting, and the wind was beginning to blow! The parka did not sufficiently protect his face.

Hugh shouted out that they were crossing a lake, and there might be a camp along its edge. They came in due course to the other side of the lake, with the cliff so steep they could not climb it. They followed the shore to the right, facing the storm. They crossed another lake, and still another. The air had grown intensely cold; the wind was higher, and ever there came that terrible inclination to lie down and sleep.

After they had passed over the last little lake Hugh shouted to John that they were surely now far from the proper trail, as he could recollect no such water near Bennett. Lake Lindeman was four miles long.

The wind was rising, and the increasing cold told that it came from the north. Hugh began now really to doubt whether they would live through the storm.

Soon afterwards fine ice crystals impinged against their faces. Great swirls of wind fell upon them. This new severe onslaught of nature aroused John, who called to his comrade. He had suddenly realized how very, very close they were to death.

"The snow is going—it's easier walking," he said suddenly.

They closed together, and struggled along abreast. They were too nearly dead to notice that the going was good. Suddenly John fell into the soft snow, and Hugh, exerting his worn powers, dragged him back.

"The trail, the trail," gasped John, with his face close to Hugh's.

"Trail! we ain't been on any trail for hours."

"Feel with your feet!"

Hugh stopped to feel with his feet two runner tracks of horse sled. Hope came to them, made a great call to their resources. Meanwhile their tired hearts and very weary bodies endured the bombardment of the snow-laden wind, which seemed to penetrate them, taking the heat of life from their vitals!

They came to another lake. How the wind cut! The snow, driven over the surface of the ice, gave a hard, grinding noise. Would ever they come to the end of that pitiless journey!

Bang! They stumbled against a sleigh standing in the middle of the road. Hugh kicked at it; the singletree rattled; he recognized the sound. He gave a desperate shout; another and another.

Then, at last, the promise of relief and of life came to them. They smelt smoke. Just for a second!—that creosotic odour was to them as sweetest perfume. It meant life, warmth, comfort, human companionship.

The figure of a man with a lantern loomed up before them, and a deep voice asked,

"What's the matter?"

"We're lost," said John.

"No, you're not; you're right here on Crater Lake, just over the summit of the Chilkoot."

"Thank God!" said Hugh.

"We're the police; come inside." They staggered into a tent warmed by a tin stove, on which was a pot of coffee. The man quickly produced cups, and gave them to drink.

John Berwick just fell on a pile of wood, stacked near the stove, and fell asleep. Now that the great struggle against the elements, which force of personality rather than strength of limbs had carried him through, was over, he collapsed.

When the policeman returned with bread and meat for them, he found Hugh removing his friend's shoes, and brushing the snow from his legs.

"Let him sleep," said Hugh.

In far-away London at that very hour—in England high noon—Alice Peel was walking down Regent Street. Her spirits were restless. The bustling traffic, the interest of the shops, the passing of the people, could not keep her thought from a far wanderer. She was weary of this ordered civilization; and remembering John in his adventures heard the call of the wilds.

There was now a possibility for this yearning to be satisfied. Her father, Surgeon-Major Peel, had lost his money through a sudden misfortune, and had been prompted by the news from the Klondike also to make a bid for fortune there, not as a gold-seeker, but in his own profession. He was convinced that a hospital in that desperate region would be in all ways a good venture.

Alice had determined to accompany him. To her that spring morning, even with all the fever of restlessness in her blood, was full of hope. The soft air and the sunshine were conditions—how different from those endured by Berwick and his comrade in their life-and-death march!

CHAPTER X
AN EMPIRE'S OUTPOST

After two hours of solid sleep, the blanket was lifted from the exhausted gold-seekers, and they were shaken back into life.

"Get up and eat, you need it."

Still aching in every bone the two poor fellows staggered to their feet.

A dim light was penetrating the canvas, as they looked about them. Underneath was ice—the frozen surface of Crater Lake—on which were spread piles of blankets, the beds of the police.

Notwithstanding the fire, the air of the tent was chill and frosty, and the canvas flapped in the wind. The walls of the tent were dark, showing the level of the snow around them. The presence of this snow, no doubt, explained how the tent had withstood the fury of the gale.

The policeman led the way to the cook tent, where they were given bacon and slap-jacks.

"Can't make bread here, and don't get it very often from Dyea, and we're just out now," apologized the policeman who acted as cook.

While they were eating ravenously, the officer in command of the post called to see them and inquired if they were any the worse for their experiences.

"Hardly salubrious, the climate, eh?" he said, after they had answered his particular questions. "On several occasions we have had the tents blown down, and frequently the men had to sit up all night holding the poles to prevent a catastrophe. I must say our fellows have shown great grit under most trying circumstances. You see we are on a civil campaign here, and there is not the excitement of fighting to keep the men up."

With that the officer left the tent. A policeman glanced after him and muttered,

"Civil campaign! Hear the old man talk! We're holding down the blooming Passes for the Queen! That's what we're doing. We could live in comfort at Lindeman, with all the wood we want for cabins and to burn."

"Where do you get your wood?"

"Down the trail—when we get any at all. They send a horse up from Lindeman. The last few days the trail has been pretty good, and some teams have been hauling from there to here: but we got only one load—which won't last us through the storm, if it holds much longer."

"Do you collect much duty here?"

"Well—rather! The old man just dumps the money he takes in a leather sack, and the other day he had thirty-five thousand dollars in it; but he hasn't got that much now. He sent one of the fellows down to Skagway with it. It was rather risky, for all the hard cases travelling the Passes got to know the sack; and there was a good deal of risk of the fellow getting shot; but he went through the whole gang and got on the boat at Dyea, and crossed to Skagway."

"The man had pluck!"

"Yes; but human nature in many ways is alike in both red-skin and white men, and the police have learned to do these sort of things. Down on the plains in the old days, when the savages were mean, it was often the case that one or two policemen would ride into a reservation, arrest a red-skin, and take him away with hundreds of armed Indians yelling around them. The Indians thought the police were crazy, and it is against their religion to kill a crazy man. I guess if Soapy recognized the sack he thought it was a job of some kind."

"Do as many men come over this Pass as over the White Pass?"

"More! The Chilkoot is the poor man's Pass. Most of the fellows who come over here haul their own stuff, and pack it over the summit, or hire the Siwashes to put it to the summit, and haul from here themselves. They get it up here, and then, when they get a fine day, run it through to Lindeman or Bennett, where they build their boats. An outfit is putting in an aerial tram: that is, a cable from the foot of the big hill to the top."

"This summit is too steep for horses?"

"Oh, yes. It's as much as an ordinary man wants to climb it light, and it's much worse with a pack on your back, though a Siwash staggered up the other day with a cask of tar weighing three hundred and fifty pounds. The sad part of it was that then he could not get his five cents, a pound for his work!—at least he came to one of our fellows, who told him to hide the barrel in the snow and not show the owner where it was, till he got his money. Wait till you see the hill! It is one of the most remarkable sights, I fancy, ever seen in the world's history: thousands of men toiling in line up nine hundred feet of almost perpendicular ascent—for what?—to be given a chance of drowning themselves in the Yukon, or of dying of disease in the Dawson country!"

The time came for the evening meal; but the storm still raged outside and the weather remained cold. It would be hard to conceive more miserable surroundings! The heat given out by the stove was scarcely felt six feet away, and the icy floor, snow walls, and flimsy roof sapped the body's heat. Darkness came, and bed-time. Two policemen offered to share their bed with the guests, so that the strangers had somewhere to lay their heads.

It appeared to John that he had just fallen to sleep when he was awakened by the sentry calling to all hands to dress, as water was overflowing the ice and coming into the tent. So up all hands got, hastily dressing in the frosty atmosphere. By the uncertain light of a few flickering candles water was to be seen entering the tent; and what was the best move was a matter of discussion, till one policeman suggested that sleighs be hauled into the tent, and the beds built on them. This was done, but not before a good portion of the bedding had become wet.

Let any one who desires a picture of the hardships which policemen and civilians went through in those dreadful Passes imagine the poor fellows living in tents, with water six inches deep within, a storm surging without—and the thermometer many degrees below freezing-point! It was three more days ere the wind ceased to blow, and for those three days the police and their guests existed under distressing conditions. At the end of the three days milder weather came; but the water still remained on the ice, so that it was plain the camp must be moved. Preparations were being made to do this when John and Hugh bade their kindly hosts good-bye.

CHAPTER XI
ANOTHER PASS

John and Hugh could not resist the temptation of looking at the far-famed Chilkoot Pass ere they turned for the last time from the Great Divide. So they mounted the steep ascent from Crater Lake to the summit. Reaching this, they found a great array of caches, or drifts of snow, the formation of which suggested a cache beneath them. A half-dozen policemen were levelling the new site for their tents.

"A desperate situation for an encampment!" said John; but there was no other.

Looking down the Pass it presented a picture like nothing so much as a great funnel, with the side towards the sea broken out. Through this passage from the sea a long line of ant-like figures, human beings, each laden with his load, was pouring towards them.

The town of Lindeman was reached at three o'clock; at five they arrived at Bennett. Dude rose up from his bed on the snow and looked at them; but the four other dogs were bundles of fur before the camp, refusing to give even a silent welcome.

"Hurrah!" cried Bruce, "here you are at last; I knew you would turn up safe and sound, so stayed home to have something hot ready."

The two were ready for another meal; and as George had set up the camp stove in the tent they were comfortable.

As soon as his partners had started on the morning of the storm, George had set to work and put up the stove in the tent, and for the balance of the day, till the storm came, had been cutting firewood—with no other idea than to keep busy. And great was his reward! for he had enough to do and to think of to keep him supplied during the storm and the severe weather that followed. Then, at seven or eight o'clock, after the snow had been falling several hours, a low wail came from outside the tent door. Dude!

"You got the note on Dude's collar?" inquired Hugh.

"Yes; but I didn't go after the grub, being too anxious about you."

"That was right. The chechachoes will have the trail beaten for us to-morrow. I only sent it in case we did not turn up, which we came pretty near not doing! How have your neighbours been getting on: doing much quarrelling?"

"No; they have had too much trouble keeping warm, and have limited their disputes as to who should go out into the storm and cut wood. They weren't as lucky as I in having a good supply at hand."

How the wanderers appreciated their warm bed under the lynx-skin robe that night! for in their late abode the chill of the ice and water had seemed to penetrate to their bones!

The next day Hugh took a piece of canvas, and with a needle fashioned a sail, after which he fixed a mast in the front of the sleigh and set the sail.

"You see," he explained, "when spring sets in the wind generally blows from the south, and we might as well make it work for us."

As it did when they started on the morning following. A breeze from the south filled the sail and helped the sleigh over the frozen surface of Lake Bennett.

It was three o'clock, and as they were close upon the end of March the days were lengthening wonderfully, so that they had not been an hour on the trail when daylight came.

As the light increased so did the wind, which relieved the dogs of almost all the weight of the load. The trail was good, and by eleven o'clock they had travelled the twenty miles to Caribou Crossing, the site of the present town of Car-Cross. Here Hugh called a halt, declaring they had done a good day's work, and that the recently-abandoned camping-ground at which they then were was too good to pass. So the dogs were unhitched, and their evening meal put to boil. While this was in process the tent was erected and the bed made.

The second day out from Lake Bennett was much like the first; and so it was until the fourth day, when they reached Miles Canyon and the White Horse rapids. From Lake Bennett they passed Windy Arm to Tagish Lake; and on Marsh Lake, which followed, they got more away from the mountains, when their range of vision became greater.

When they arrived at the foot of Marsh Lake, which merged into Miles Canyon, they found a number of men putting in a tramway, over which horses would haul freight when navigation opened, thus covering the five miles and avoiding the danger of the canyon and the rapids.

They hauled their load along the route of the tramway to below the rapids, where the waters of the Yukon are known as the Fifty Mile River. Here they found a number of men building boats, but they kept steadily on.

Below White Horse Rapids fewer men were on the trail. Some they met were travelling south, gaunt and haggard, unshaven, uncouth, loud of voice and wild of eye. These men had travelled the long trail from Dawson—five hundred miles it was; and the heavy toil and hard food had told on their minds and natures.

The party covered the fifteen miles from White Horse to where the Fifty Mile enters Lake Le Berge, when the crust had become so soft that they could not travel, so they camped. Recently the trail had taken on new conditions, that of standing higher than the snow on either hand, like the back of a great serpent. The fact was that the general level of snow was settling under the warmth of the sun, while the trail, being packed hard, remained as it was.

The tent was up and the bed made by noon. Hugh planned that the party should go to bed at three, and "hit the trail" again at midnight. There would be no wind to aid them further, for, as they left the coast range, the diurnal breeze had failed. Their own efforts, and those of the dogs, must haul the load the final stage of thirty miles to the foot of Lake Le Berge, where they were to build their boat.

They ate their dinner and spread spruce boughs, over which they placed their blankets, and enjoyed a rest in the glorious sunlight.

The view from the tent was beautiful. To the north lay the stretch of the lake, on either hand of which were great rounded hills—all dazzling white. To the south, far distant, were heavy ranges of mountains. The air was that of peace and hope, and seemed full of promise of the glorious summer soon to burst over this vastness of solitude, melting the snows, and flooding the hillsides with floral beauty.

Presently they saw two black specks crossing the frozen lake far beneath, which eventually proved to be two human figures approaching—one some distance behind the other. The first was hauling a sled, slowly, and evidently with difficulty. Hugh at once acted. He put the kettle to boil, and filled a frying-pan with beans and bacon.

"I guess those fellows coming up the lake will need a little grub when they get here," he explained; "at least they can drink tea, if they are too plumb played out to eat."

The actions of the leading man were very erratic. Frequently he would stop, place his hand before his eyes, and when again he endeavoured to start would stagger, plunging into the softened snow, which broke under him, bringing him to the knees.

"Snow-blind," was Hugh's comment.

The stranger seemed to smell the smoke from the camp fire, and gave a wild "Hullo!" The three answered the call. He turned towards the sound, and when he saw the camp he shook himself free of the harness and plunged through the soft snow towards it. When he saw the blankets stretched before the tent he threw himself on them at full length, and with his fingers at his eye-sockets groaned.

Sympathy being often better expressed by doing nothing, the man was left in his misery for some ten minutes. Hugh then poured him out a cup of tea, to which was added much sugar and condensed milk. The man raised his head at a word, and showed his blackened face, made horrible by the streaks of tears and perspiration. He drank the refreshment greedily. Hugh explained the man's curious appearance.

"This fellow has been taking a leaf out of the Siwash's book in blackening his face. The black saves the eyes a whole lot from the glare of the sun."

The campers turned their attention to the second traveller, now plainly in sight, and noticed that the pack on his back jolted him horribly, as he broke through the trail at every third or fourth step. As he wore glasses, he was evidently not in distress from his eyes. He saw the camp, staggered to it, and threw himself down, pack and all, sitting with his back against the load. He stared at the man in agony on the blankets.

"Hello! there's Bill! Ha! I told the blame fool not to travel without glasses. Wake up, Bill, and tell us your dreams. How's that wife you're so struck on outside, and you in such a hurry to give your dust to! Ho! Bill, wake up!"

As the prostrate man gave no sign of hearing, his hilarious companion turned to the others, and in more moderate tones continued,

"Bill and me have come from Dawson together, and he has near killed himself—me, too—trying to get out and see his wife and kids; and this morning nothing would do him but he must go and tramp on his glasses, and bust them. I told him to lay up to-day and travel to-night, but he wouldn't. Must keep moving to get to his wife. Ha! Wife be damned! I ain't got no wife."

Hugh interrupted the tirade.

"Have some beans?"

"Sure thing! Beans—yes; nothing like beans on the trail; besides, I don't mind eating your beans, seeing my own grub pile is most petered out. Just a little flour and baking-powder left; not much good to travel on."

The man fell to eating. His manner turned from hilarity to morosity. He bolted his food. Soon his companion on the blankets moved, and gasped, "Don't let that hog eat all the beans; I want some."

"Ha! I thought Bill wasn't dead: you're just a bluffer, ain't you, Bill? Say! Bill, let's turn round and go back to Dawson. We can travel along with these fellows: they have lots of grub, and we can buy off them."

It was evident to John and his friends that—if the first stranger was the worse affected in physical condition—the second was mentally the more upset. The snow-blinded sufferer raised himself and took from Hugh the plate of beans and a second cup of tea. This man ate slowly, while his partner continued to talk.

"You see, me and Bill came from Dawson together; and when we got to Thirty Mile we found it open, and the blame sleigh was always sliding into the open water. I wanted Bill to chuck the sleigh and pack our grub and blankets; but Bill wouldn't. So I says, 'I'll pack my half, and you can haul your half,' and that's the way we've been coming. Bill had a hell of a time with his sleigh sliding into the river; and then, coming up the lake, he never could keep it on the trail. No wonder he's bughouse!"[7]

[7] Crazy.

When the first arrival had finished his meal Hugh led him into the tent and bathed his eyes with fresh-made tea. In the tent the sufferer was free from the glare of the sun. Hugh hung a dark grey blanket from the ridge pole, so that if the sufferer opened his eyes he could fix his gaze upon it. Then he went out.

"How's Bill?" asked the erratic one.

"Better, I hope."

"Not bughouse yet?"

"I don't think so."

"Well, if he ain't bughouse, he is sure locoed on that wife of his."

Hugh made no reply, and the other continued,

"Ha! that's Bill Stanbridge; owns in on Eldorado with Slim Mulligan, who's in charge now, and will look after the clean-up. My name is Frank Miller; just blew in about the time Carmack made discovery, but went and used my rights on Boulder Creek. Boulder showed up better on surface than Bonanza or Eldorado, but there's nothing on bed-rock in Boulder."

As the man got his mind away from his partner, his conversation indicated less disorder of intellect. Hugh, quickly noticing the change, and with a view to further the good process, asked,

"How's Dawson?"

"Dawson! She's fine. Lots of grub. Old Healey gave the boys a speel last fall that they'd all starve if they stayed in the country, and then the speculators corralled all the grub and run up prices; but they're loosening now. You can get a pretty good meal of beans now for two dollars and a half—even at Miss Mulrooney's. Say! that girl is making money."

"How's Bonanza?"

"Good; but Eldorado is better. Bill's go ground, some of it going five hundred dollars to the pan for picked dirt. But this high grade pay! The Government is going to send their yellow-legs round to relieve the boys of ten per cent., and fellows with poor ground will have to pay as well as the fellows on Eldorado. That ain't fair!"

"It's fair to charge for the administration of the country and keeping law and order," said George.

"To hell with law and order! You're a chechacho, or you wouldn't talk like that. Miners' meetings make pretty good law-courts; and now they have law and order, fellows begin to lock their doors. The country was a whole lot better before ever it saw an official."

"Yes; but the gang going in now will make things different," said Hugh.

"You're an old-timer?... Thought so when I first swallowed your beans. Chechachoes don't know how to boil beans like that. You'll find a big change round Rabbit Creek when you blow in there. It's gamblers and saloon men most have the good claims. Of course Carmack had to put his wife's relations in next to him on discovery; and when the crowd got up from Forty Mile they staked on Boulder Gulch and Adams Gulch. Neither any good—but say! they've got Dawson a hot town." He laughed. "Games running night and day; all the fun you want, but no gun-play; the yellow-legs will put you on the wood-pile right away quick, if ever you make a break; and it ain't no fun to be sawing wood at forty below, with a yellow-legs and a Winchester standing over you—for the glory of the Queen of England!"

Frank Miller's mind was lapsing.

CHAPTER XII
A NEW PARTNER

Frank Corte stood at the door of his kitchen and, with a large smile, eyed the coming of the party. The new-comers were evidently going to build their boat at the foot of Le Berge; and already he had favourably sized them up.

There were many tents pitched around the cabin where Frank distributed the necessities of human sustenance; but Dude's instincts drew him to the kitchen, and down he and his canine followers flopped before the door.

"Well! well! fine dogs, nice day, strangers. Going to build boat here? yes, thought so. Thirty Mile is open to the Hootalink, and the Lewis is getting holes in it. Early spring, sure!"

Frank's heart was hospitable; but the cost of grub was high: moreover, the grub he cooked was not his. He was debating how far his hospitality could go.

Frank Corte was a Hungarian by birth, and a citizen of the United States of America, which he proudly announced as opportunity offered. He was over six feet tall, with long arms, stooping shoulders, and an angular form. His physical strength was enormous: there was a wealth of native kindness in his heart. His chief diversion was argument, in which—thanks to his study of the Bible, and a small, besmeared pocket-edition of Webster's Dictionary—he was rather effective. He could argue with any one; or even on necessity address his convictions to the little red-haired female dog that was ever at his heels. Frank thought the world of Fanny.

"Say! fellows, it's against orders to feed pilgrims, though I guess you ain't altogether tenderfeet; but if you wants to boil your tea and cook grub on my stove, you're welcome. Come right in and cook up."

"No, thanks," said Hugh, "though I guess I will leave the team here and mooch round and get a good camping-place. I guess we'll be here three weeks, and might as well set up our tent in a good place. We're not hungry."

"That's right; and you can't have a better camping-ground than right over against that bunch of spruce." Frank was interested in these strangers, and his desire for news stimulated his hospitality; so he continued, "Come right in and feed up, and look for your camping-ground after. Days are getting long now."

Hugh hesitated, and then accepted. Frank put on more wood, to which the tin stove quickly responded.

"How's Soapy?" he inquired.

"Fine," replied Hugh, "hold-ups galore. The people of Skagway have a murder nearly every morning for breakfast!"

"Say! what a time Soapy would have if they only let him operate around Dawson—wouldn't he make a killing! But them police! They don't have any more excitement beyond the games and dance-halls in Dawson than they do outside. That's no mining-camp for a country like this, and the crowd what's inside there now. I don't like to see too much killing, but a hold-up now and again is interesting!—besides, these rich claim-owners can stand it. A fellow was telling me that it was nothing to see the 'Big Moose'[8] coming into Dawson, last summer, with ten or twenty thousand dollars tied to his saddle, and him without a guard! Say! we're going to have a squaw-dance Friday night in the dining-room here, will you come? One of our fellows has an accordion, and we'll have fine music. Only four bits a dance. I'm going to try and get some hootch. There's nothing like hootch to get the squaws on the move—if the yellow-legs don't get on to it. They soak you like the devil if they catch you at it, though. Say! how's Uncle Sam getting on licking them there Spaniards?—he'll do them up in about three weeks. I'd like to be outside to go to the Philippines. After he gets through with the Spaniards he's going to come in and take Canada,"—and here Frank stole side-glances at Hugh's companions; but his instincts of hospitality stayed him from this, his favourite joke.

[8] Indian name for the late Alexander McDonald.

"Say! where did you get those dogs? Fine team!"

"Three I got inside; the others in Skagway."

"I thought you was no chechacho. You come from Uncle Sam's country, don't you?"

"I come from all over: what's this outfit you're with?"

"Jack Haskins is building two scows to take down some freight he hauled in over the ice. He has me cooking for him, though I could get $250.00 in Dawson for the same job. He only pays me $150.00 per month; but I'll soon be in with the best of them. Say! if you fellows is going to build a boat, I'll ask Jack if you can't use one of his pits. He has two, and I guess you fellows can get the chance to use one of his pits for all the lumber you want—and that will save you building one. I'm glad you fellows have showed up—it will make more company—and I hope you'll come to our dance. You'll see the squaw-camp down the river a bit. They're out from Dalton House, came out to Tagish, visiting some Siwashes there, and drifted down here, just to take in the sights! Are a bit shy, though some have picked up a little English."

"Here is another human study," thought John, as he and his friends moved over to the point suggested for their encampment. They found it satisfactory, so went back for the dogs.

"Say! if you fellows want anything in the way of dishes, or if you're real short of any grub, maybe I can let you have it on the sly," said Frank to the party as they returned, his hospitality getting ahead of his morals. But Hugh assured him the party was fixed up all right.

Frank's generosity was of the aggressive kind, for as John Berwick's party sat in their tent that evening he stuck his head in at the door and said they could have the use of one of Haskins' saw-pits on the morrow, and probably right along.

"Don't work too hard, for I want you to be lively on Friday night! Two fellows have just blown in from Dawson, and they say the river is full of holes; so it is just as well you fellows don't have to build a pit; it looks like an early opening, maybe about the first of May."

"The river won't open by the first of May, but it will before the tenth, most likely," commented Hugh.

Next morning the party visited the yard where the scows were building, and introduced themselves to Mr. Haskins, who again informed them that the saw-pits were at their disposal when he did not require them.

"Ever do any whip-sawing?" asked Haskins.

"Some," said Hugh.

"It's no picnic."

"I never found it so. How's timber? That looks pretty good up the hill there," and Hugh pointed to a clump of spruce.

"Yes, it's all right; but you'll find bigger and clearer stuff higher up, and you can mush it down the hill easy. I suppose you have your own saw?"

With this the three friends stormed the hill. They were to cut the trees and slide them to the bottom, after which the dogs would aid in hauling them to the pit. The trees Hugh selected were the larger ones, clean and free from knots. By the close of the day sufficient logs were at the pit.

A saw "pit" is a scantling of poles eight feet high, on which the logs are placed to be sawn. The *modus operandi* is that one man stands below the log and another on the top: the upper man pulls the saw towards him, the lower man co-operates. The work is simplicity itself, but very hard. The three companions would want from two to three hundred feet of lumber, which meant perspiration and backache. As Hugh expressed it, "the upper man is up against about the hardest proposition a white man puts himself at, these days."

About three o'clock on the first afternoon of whip-sawing Frank Corte appeared with Fanny at his heels. George was the upper man, and even his elastic muscles were aching at the work. Hugh was having a spell off, but keeping an eye on his friends.

"Ha! how do you fellows like hard work? This will teach you to go hunting after gold! What have you done with your last summer's wages? Say! we're going to have a great time at the dance—a regular potlatch: one of the Sticks has just come in saying he's killed a caribou back on the hills, and is going to potlatch it. Now if I can only get some hootch! I'd give ten dollars a bottle for some."

"Better cut the hootch out," said Hugh. "The police may catch you and send you down to Dawson; and put you sawing wood for Queen Victoria. And it won't be Uncle Sam's men who will be chasing you with a Winchester."

"Yes, yes. A damned pity Uncle Sam would not come over and take Canada: then we should have a camp at Dawson."

George was very hot and sore; and this sort of bantering was new to him. He was in that humour which causes a man to go into a fight on little provocation; but John, he noticed, was smiling amicably, so he held his peace.

"If this was Uncle Sam's country, Soapy would have been here taking away your wages before this," laughed Hugh.

"I wouldn't kick if he could do the trick. Say! can you dance? This is going to be a swell dance all right! Wish I had enough lumber to cover the floor, so we could dance proper. Poles is mighty hard to dance on. Well, I must be going—I have some beans boiling. Don't you fellows tire yourselves too much sawing lumber, so you can't dance to-morrow night."

CHAPTER XIII
THE DANCE

"Are you all set? Then dance! damn you, dance! Come on, gentlemen, get partners for the next."

Frank Corte's great dance was on. Hugh and his companions stood by the door of the dining-hall. On went the dance; and through the atmosphere—thick with tobacco-smoke—the native women were guided, their bronzed faces speaking excitement.

"Come on in, gentlemen!"

The walls of the room were lined with men. Squaws, who had not yet learned the dance, sat on boxes. The three friends crowded into the room and stood with their backs against the wall. Frank Corte was beating time with his foot and clapping his hands, while he sang the calls in a weird drawl.

"Honours to the right." Each man bowed most gravely to his partner, who most respectfully returned it. "Honours to the left." Each man bowed to the lady at his left in the quadrille: and when "Swing your right-hand lady; dance around the room" came, the men grabbed their partners and whirled around—quarters were too close to permit of any great range of movement, and the squaws were so excited, they seemed to occupy more room than really they did.

"A la main left." All stood to attention. "First gent swing the left-hand lady, with the left hand round."

Every gentleman turned towards the lady on his left. The ladies turned to the right. They grasped left hands at the height of their shoulders, and pranced round to the left.

"The left hand round.—Turn your partners, with the right hand, round.—The right hand round.—All chassez!—First couple lead to the right.—Four hand round.—Dos à balnette.—Right hand to partner, and grand dos à balnette." Every man took his partner's right hand and wheeled to the right; and then her left hand. This movement brought them opposite, and so they were in a circle, at which they balanced, the men facing outwards, the women inwards.

"On to the next!"

The men wheeled, and with their ladies pivoted to the left; then the men took the hand of the ladies next on their right as they swung round. The ladies holding the men by the left gave their right hand, and at the words "dos à balnette," all again balanced—the men this time facing inwards, the ladies outwards.

"On the next!"—again brought the men facing outwards, the ladies inwards—and so on. The quadrille was concluded with,

> "Promenade all
> Around the hall,
> And seat your ladies at the ball."

The faces of the crowd were wild with excitement. The music was weird and discordant. Yet John found it all very stimulating. Dance after dance was gone through, while he stayed and watched, till there came to his mind pictures of the old home—his father's house in London, and Alice Peel! Was she thinking of him?

"Say! why don't you fellows get in and dance?"

Dreams and fancies were reft away as reality, in the person of Haskins of the saw-pits, stood before John Berwick. Then he noticed George laughing at a clumsy mystified squaw, a beginner in the dance. His hilarity provoked the squaw, and, as the dance paused for a second, between her gasps and through her perspiration she hissed with a look of contempt,

"Che—chac. Ka!"

"Say! you fellows will have to get in and dance in this next set. I saw a squaw looking at you and saying 'heap dam dood,' so if you want to keep your station in society you've got to dance." Haskins was again worrying them.

"All right. Who will I ask to dance?" George was ready.

"Go and ask that squaw sitting in the corner," said Haskins, pointing across the room. She it was who had said "Heap dam dood."

George went and invited her to be his partner.

"Ni—ka halo introdux" (You have not been introduced), she answered.

This was more than George could withstand in gravity. He roared with laughter and returned to Haskins. He only guessed the meaning of the words, so he repeated them to Haskins.

"Who the devil has taught these savages up here chinook! It's a special lingo manufactured by the Hudson Bay Company to suit the savages, and when white men first came into British Columbia they found the savages with a lingo which was called white man's wa-wa, and which no person could understand; it is easy enough to learn, you can pick it up in a week; it has only about six hundred words. All the old-timers in British Columbia talk it. Dagoes, Chinese, Mexicans, Swedes, all talked it in the old days in Caribou. The Siwash calls an Englishman 'King George man' and an American 'Boston man.'"

The squaw in the corner was keeping her eye on George with evident dislike. As John noticed this he recommended their departure; so George and he went back to bed. Hugh arrived home hours later in great glee.

"You fellows will laugh at the Siwashes, eh? Well—you'll get the worst of it. George, I hear you were not sufficiently formal with one of the klootches (squaws), and got called down—ha, ha!"

On the Sunday morning following John left Hugh and George repairing their wardrobe in the tent, and was strolling past Frank Corte's kitchen to where the scows were being built.

"Hullo! how's the 'heap dam dood'? Come in, I want to argue with you."

John looked up and saw the smiling face of Frank at his kitchen door. He had no great wish to argue; but he loved the study of humanity, and realized that Frank was something of a conundrum.

Corte, who was kneading bread, took a seat on a box by the kitchen door.

"Say! don't you think it would be a good thing for this country if Uncle Sam was really to come over and take it?"

"I hope not. What's the matter with it as it is?"

"Too much police—too much law and order; you can never have a real live mining-camp in Canada."

"That was a pretty good dance you had Friday night."

"Yes, it was all right; but what a time we would have had if we had had lots of hootch! But say! that was a good one when the squaw told the other 'King George man' he had not been introduced to her!"

Frank chuckled; and then, as the prospect of an international argument did not seem good, went on another tack.

"Do you believe there is a God?"

A flood of memories surged through Berwick's brain.

He glanced at the dark sinister features of the man awaiting his reply and then looked at the sunlight. Should he give such an answer in such a tone as would discourage further argument? No—the question was too serious. He might not have felt called upon at one time to divulge his belief, which in the past had been a burden of much questioning; but here it was asked, perhaps in levity, by one who evidently could not fully believe. He felt called upon to answer,

"Yes, I do."

Corte's face had taken on a strained look. Realizing the seriousness with which Berwick regarded the question, he feared lest he had hurt the feelings of his guest. The answer he received reassured him. Removing his big arms from the dough, and gesticulating, he answered,

"Well, partner, I don't. Now here's the proposition: those who say there is a God say what He set out to do. The first thing God done was to build the world; and after He done this He built a mighty fine ranch and fixed it up A1; and then He puts Adam and Eve into it, after having made them. He tells them not to eat apples—and then He goes and has a snake which tells them to eat apples. And because they do eat apples He pulls up the ranch and kicks them out. Now there would be no kick coming if He simply turned them loose and made them rustle—having to rustle never hurt any man—but He brings all sorts of diseases and pains on earth. That's what keeps me from believing in God.

"Now look here; if God was able to make the earth, and the stars, and everything, why should He not make man and let him enjoy all this—seeing that He is doing it all more or less for amusement—without putting him in the middle of a lot of good things and then putting up a job on him? I've talked to parsons on this thing, and some of them says that after He bust up the home ranch He kind of got sorry, and says He would send His Son on earth to die—to fix up the big mistake Adam and Eve made in eating one apple. Now, say! If you was doing all this, would you, after you made man, and put him on the earth and he did wrong, would you send your son to fix things up so that the crowd would go and nail him to a big wooden cross by driving big stakes through his hands and feet—and then stick him up for the crows to peck at? If God was not able to make a man the first go off who would stand a mill-test, why did He not kill him off, body and soul, and try again without trying to fix things up by making His Son suffer? The whole proposition ain't natural. And what would you think of a man who, if he fell down on any proposition, would make his son go and suffer to fix up his mistakes? Why did He not come on earth and die on the cross Himself, and suffer, and turn the earth and all the stars and the rest of it over to His Son to run while He was gone?"

John Berwick was not by nature argumentative, having seldom in his life allowed himself to be drawn into any but political controversy. He had, it is true, discussed doctrine at college with his class-mates. He had read much philosophy, and had pondered deeply on the mystery of human suffering—the deepest of all mysteries. He had weighed the arguments of great minds which wanted belief in God, and in his own mind had done much to surmount the difficulty, to justify the ways of God to man; but the crude intellect before him had launched forth a proposition he could not confute. His training in rhetoric and in the drawing of parallels was of use only against the cultured mind. The legend of the Saxon king drawing the simile of life from the little bird which flew within the hall firelight and was gone again came to his mind, but he put it aside as impotent. He did not know what to say; he said nothing.

Frank Corte was working at his bread again, his face twitching with a smile.

"And then there's miskities, and black flies, and moose flies, and bull-dogs. Say! wait a month or two till the miskities get busy, and then try and figure out how any great and good God would put such things on earth! These devils ain't in cities where men is, but in the country where the beasts is. Have you ever seen a big bull-moose going hell-bent for election through the bush chased by flies? Have you ever shot a bear, with his eyes and ears and nose full of flies, and the flies sticking all round his eyes, enough to drive even a bear plumb crazy? Why should God, because man went and eat an apple, make animals suffer in trying to get even?"

Frank Corte returned to the kneading, while John Berwick thoughtfully watched the sun-flooded landscape.

"Frank," he said, after a pause, "'the proof of the pudding is the eating.' I have never heard any argument quite like yours, but man's coming to the world, how he came to the world, and whether he has a soul have been the greatest subjects of study through the ages. We know the Christian religion was taught back to within a few years of the time Christ came on earth; and from that time on has got bigger in power and influence over the minds of men, so that the majority of civilized people give justice to their fellows because this religion tells them to do so.

"The Bible tells a story of the origin of man, which we may or may not believe. The Bible says there is a God; and God sees best not to explain His schemes and why He makes man and animals suffer. I believe there is a God, and that God is just, and that there is a reason for everything. Why not try to believe there is a God, rather than argue with yourself and others that there is no God? If the Christian belief has made the world so much better as a whole, it will make you and me better as single men; and I know you would give a man a meal if he wanted it; or if a fellow were sick you would help him out all you could, and you'd expect me to do the same. If you saw a fellow drowning in the river you'd help him out; but the Chinaman, who is not a Christian, would let him drown. You're a Christian all right; but you don't know it."

John paused, and would have added something; but Frank, his face half flushed in confusion, his voice less rasping than usual, broke in,

"Say! stranger, when I first saw you I sized you up along with the Siwashes as a 'heap dam dood,' though I didn't like to say it serious-like; but that's a pretty good talk of yours, and, sure, sounds natural. Say! is that other 'King George man' with you as good a fellow as you are? Say! you've set me thinking!"

Frank had set Berwick thinking too.

CHAPTER XIV
A LONG SHOT

Hugh Spencer was working as upper man on the whip-saw, and an Indian was trying to extract a cartridge from an old and rusty rifle at his camp down the river. Suddenly there was a report, and Hugh tumbled headlong from his position. His friends sprang to his side, and found blood spurting from a hole in his neck.

The flow was not great, so that their first feeling of horror was changed to hopefulness. John shouted and waved to Haskins, whom he saw standing near his scows. Haskins came running up, was told what had happened, and with the single word, "Wait!" bolted to his tent. He was back again in little more than a minute, with a camp-bed, blankets and all. Few words were spoken, and those in whispers. The injured man was lifted on to the bed, and carried to the tent, his temporary home.

"George, hot water." George was off to the cook-tent at the word, while Haskins got Hugh on his side, the wound uppermost, and Frank arrived hurriedly.

"Boracic acid out of the medicine bag; Frank, you light the fire, and then take off Hugh's boots."

"It don't look as if it was bad," said Haskins, when the wound was washed.

"No," replied John, "I don't think the bullet is far in, it is the shock that has knocked him out; but I have no instruments with which to get the bullet out, and even if I were able to draw it, it might be followed by a rush of blood I should not know how to stop; and then there is the danger of blood poisoning."

"A doctor with his partner is building a boat at White Horse," said Haskins.

"Good! I'll get him! George, you know what to do. Keep a good watch, and when he comes round keep him quiet."

John left the tent, and saw four of the dogs before Frank's kitchen.

"See anything of Dude?" he called to Frank.

"Yes, he was in front of my kitchen all the afternoon." Frank looked out of the tent door. "Say! I've left my door open. I bet he's stole something!" They ran to look. "Yes, a side of bacon's gone. Damn that 'dood'—'heap dam dood,' he!" Frank's sense of humour could not be suppressed by any calamity; but its expression did not stay his activities. He was out of his kitchen and peering into the bushes on the hillside.

"Yes, I thought so; there he is, been up to his cache I located the other day; he's done quick work and is coming back. Don't call him, he'll come quicker without, and he may think we want to lick him for thieving. Come inside."

It seemed an age before the reprobate reappeared before the cabin.

"Don't let on you see him, but walk by and grab him," whispered Frank.

John followed the instructions and was successful.

"Where's the harness?" asked Frank.

"With the sleigh at the tent. I'll get it."

"Here, Two Bits; here, Four Bits; here, Tom, Jerry," and Frank had the team in harness. "Dude!"

Dude went to his place in the lead.

"Hold on a minute."

Frank went into the kitchen, and returned with half a loaf of bread and some fried bacon, in a piece of birch bark.

"Throw this into you as you go."

"How about the dogs?"

"Damn the dogs; I've been feeding them all day."

"Mush!"

Dude looked back and did not move.

"Mush!" He moved ahead at a slow walk.

"Mush, damn you!" John felt surprised to hear himself swear; but the dogs were in the condition styled "ornery." Dude turned in by the side of the building, the others followed; the sleigh bumped against the corner. Frank had Dude by the collar in a moment, and was belabouring him over the flank with a stout stick. The hills reverberated with howls. He hauled the animals back into line, and with a kick for good measure, said in a cold slow tone,

"Mush."

Dude trotted off. Frank ran by the side of the team till they were on the lake. "They'll go all right if you once get them away from camp, but lick 'em good and plenty if they turn mean," was his counsel on quitting.

John Berwick was alone with the team on the great expanse of Lake Le Berge. Before him, to the south, lay the thirty-mile stretch of ice, flanked by rolling hills, flooded with opalescent tints and peace. For an instant the exceeding beauty of the scene gladdened his mind.

He was anxious about Hugh. There were forty-five miles to traverse before he would come to White Horse. The dogs were travelling at five miles an hour: nine hours before he could reach White Horse; and then, if the river were open, what then? The thought of the delay necessitated by a journey overland staggered him. It were easier to travel thirty miles on the ice than fifteen through the bush. He jumped off the sleigh and ran; but the dogs moved no faster; and the labour in running would soon exhaust him, for while there was no snow on the ice, the surface of the lake was a coarse ice-sand, which constituted a poor foothold. The sun was setting; already a chill was in the air. A crust would form within the hour; perhaps the dogs would move faster then.

These thoughts ran through his mind, till his fear developed into a lingering dread. He realized that to go through that intolerable process of analyzing the details of his anxiety could only result in futility. The surface of the lake became harder; he picked up pieces of ice, threw them at Dude, and shouted. Every missile, with its accompanying shout, brought a merely temporary increase of speed. All attempts to get the dogs to gallop proved futile.

It was three o'clock on the following morning when Berwick pounded on the door of the police cabin at White Horse, and was greeted sleepily.

He entered. The flicker of a match showed a man in the act of lighting a candle by the head of a bed built against the wall.

"Man shot at the foot of Le Berge; bullet in his neck; wants doctor."

The policeman jumped from bed, slipped to the door, and pointed to a tent by the river-side.

"The doctor with his partner live in that tent. What is it—accident?"

"Yes; Indian trying to extract a cartridge from an old rifle."

"Damn the Siwashes! Same old story. Well, I have no doubt the doctor will go. I guess you'll need some sleep, so if those fellows can't put you up, return here, and you can climb into bed with me."

John had intended returning to his friend with the doctor, but bolted without comment, save a mere "Thank you."

There is no process of knocking at a tent door, so John used his voice to rouse the occupants.

"What do you want?" was the gruff response.

John gave the necessary information.

"Doc," then said the man to his unseen companion, "there's a chance of doing the Good Samaritan act the preachers talk about."

There was silence for a while as the doctor and his comrade were dressing and preparing; then John asked,

"Can I build a fire outside and cook some dog feed? If you will let me have some feed I'll return it, or pay for it."

"I thought you was a chechacho!" said the gruff voice. "You want the Doc to travel quick?"

"Certainly."

"And the Doc's taking them dogs home?"

"Yes."

"Well, don't feed them."

John Berwick's nature revolted against this theory; but he made no protest, as the life of his mate was in jeopardy.

The doctor packed his hand-bag, and was ready.

"You stay here," he said; "you can do no good down there. Roll in and have a sleep."

Dude was alert, but the other dogs were in repose when they were jerked into life again. The train moved down the river. Fatigued in body and mind, Berwick gladly rested and slept.

CHAPTER XV
REVELATION

John awoke at five in the afternoon. At the first opportunity his new acquaintance began to talk.

"My name's Jim Godson. 'Shorty' the boys call me; sometimes 'Long-Shorty.' That's what you call a blooming paradox, ain't it, Parson?"

"I'm not a parson."

"Well, if you ain't, you look as if you ought to be. What's your name?... Oh, is it?... Ain't you got no appellation yet?"

"Not as yet."

"Well, I'll call you Parson Jack, though I guess you look too good a man for a parson. Parsons is mostly parsons because they're too lazy to work; and you don't act lazy. No, you ain't lazy; not if you are in tow with an old-timer."

Godson's light chatter kept away the sense of apprehension which was ever tending to creep into Berwick's mind.

"Say! I knew a parson once that was worth having. Yes, sir; Father Pat was his name, and his run was down in the Kootenays. A whiter parson never lived than Father Pat."

"Father Pat? Was he a Roman Catholic? The Roman clergy are not called 'parsons.'"

"No, sir; he weren't no Catholic; he was an Angle (Anglican)—and a pretty acute one, too. He was moseying along a trail down below one day, and was just turning off on a side-trail leading to a mining proposition up there, when three fellows met him, who were just naturally full of cussedness. 'How do?' says Father Pat. 'Where are you going?' says the fellows. 'I'm going up to the mine,' says Father Pat. 'No, you ain't,' says the fellows. 'But I am,' says Father Pat. 'We don't want no damned parsons around here,' says the fellows. 'I can't help that,' says Father Pat, 'I'm going up the hill; and if you fellows want to quarrel over it, I'll take you one at a time and lick you.' And he did so. Now that's what I call a parson worth having."

"And which of the three were you?" asked John.

"Me! I was the second fellow that got licked; yes, since then I've always thought parsons worth looking into."

The time for departure came.

"Go easy for the first two or three miles, Parson; forty-five miles is a pretty good walk for any fellow who ain't an old-timer. You're making a mistake not waiting, for the dogs will be back here with the doctor, even if he has to stay a day or two with your partner; but if you're stuck on going, I guess I ain't got any string on you."

"Good-bye," said John, and clambered down the river-bank to the ice.

The day had been more than usually warm, the air unusually clear; the evening frost had come early.

As Berwick left White Horse it was seven, and already the crust had formed. He had food in his pockets, and the air brought him stimulation. Anxiety steeled his muscles. Away he strode.

He passed from the curving river, and came again to the frozen stretch of Lake Le Berge. The light of day was gone; the stars gleamed and danced, and shed their glamour over the hills. And what dignity they held! Greece had risen and gone to decay: Cæsar had striven after his great ambition: Pharaoh had succeeded Pharaoh: while those hills had slept as they now were sleeping.

The influence of his environment closed upon John Berwick. The psychic force of the weird Northland was upon him. Through his mind passed the orthodox story of creation; and, again and again, as he walked, he weighed the various arguments of the agnostic. He looked upon the limestone masses to the east, and mused upon the ways of Nature, which caused the destruction of myriads of shell-fish to upbuild the marble of the palace. He pictured the diamond in the atomic theory of matter—a mass of pulsating atoms oscillating within magnetic bonds—even as the stars swing through space, guided by the influence which is called gravitation. Was not this known movement of the heavenly bodies similar to the theoretic movement of the atom?

A feeling of apprehension grew in John Berwick; faster and faster he walked. Life's greatest problems had for years occupied his mind. He looked about him and into the heavens. Before his fevered eyes the stars shimmered and grew in shape: the earth beneath him dwindled and melted, till it was but a star and he felt its rush through space. He realized the centrifugal force that would throw the world out of its orbit; he felt the counteracting restraint; system joined to system, swinging, circling, driving; the universe grew about him; suns and stars were but atoms in a component whole; the whole formed into Presence—Love! God!

It came to him as a mighty magnificent discovery.

He must hurry to tell Frank Corte!

CHAPTER XVI
A STREAM OF HISTORY

"Good-bye, fellows, wish you all kinds of luck! I won't be long behind you."

"Good-bye," answered the four from the boat that glided out on the swift waters of Thirty-Mile River. In the bow stood Hugh Spencer, bandaged; at the oars were Bruce and Frank Corte; in the stern John Berwick, pale and weak from his late fever, was resting. A new light shone in his eyes; the lines of his face were softened. Anxieties which had been as a weight on his soul had been removed by that revealing walk, which had ended in catastrophe.

He had been found by the side of the trail some few hours after he had fallen in delirium. The legs of his trousers were worn at the knees; his flesh was cut through his struggling after he had fallen. His finger-tips were worn to the quick; his blood had stained the ice.

The doctor, returning, had been John's rescuer, and had placed him on the sleigh. Truly a good Samaritan, he had returned with the invalid to the foot of Le Berge.

Berwick's delirium was the climax of half-a-dozen years of mental strain. His old struggle as to whether he should make his vocation in the Church, as well as his almost hopeless passion for Alice Peel, had, though even George Bruce barely suspected it, wrought upon him. Now the climax had come; and was passed.

George, seeing this catastrophe, had guessed much; the doctor, trained in the study of humanity, had also guessed something. Hugh, Frank Corte, and Haskins only knew that John had played-out on the trail.

Spencer had told his companions there was nothing much in the first six miles of the river, but that afterwards "she is swift and crooked." Sunken boulders were the chief danger, so he took his post in the bow to "read" the water ahead, and to direct the course, saying "Frank" or "George"—as he wished the one or the other to pull the harder.

After an hour the boat came to a point where the river takes a turn to the right, on rounding which the boat's pace increased. Looking over its side into the clear water, John saw the stones at the bottom flash by, and noted the scurrying greyling affrighted.

The boat swept by sunken boulders, or grazed the curving shores, but held its swift course without pause or incident. For four hours their rapid progress continued; then the current died away, and the boat floated upon the dead water that marks the junction of the Hootalinquia River with the Thirty Mile, henceforth to be called the Lewis, till Lewis is joined by the Pelly to become the Yukon.

Now that the necessity for vigilance was past, Hugh entertained his friends with reminiscences of his first trip there, and the story of the entrance of the gold-seekers to the Upper Yukon. They would soon be at Cassiar Bar, and the mouth of the Big Salmon River. In 1881 miners had crossed the Passes, and descended the lakes and rivers, to the mouth of the Big Salmon, which they ascended, and obtained gold by washing the bars. Cassiar Bar was not discovered till 1886, five years after the Big Salmon party had done their mining. The men who mined Cassiar Bar had wintered here, and their cabin came in useful for others who "mushed out" over the ice to give word about Howard Franklin's discovery of coarse gold on the Forty Mile, and to order more grub to be sent "up river" by the Alaska Commercial Company's steamer. In 1880 some fellows from Sitka had gone over, and prospected up the Hootalinquia; but they did not strike much; while the first white man over the Passes looking for gold was George Holt, who found a few "colours" around Lake Bennett. In 1873 Arthur Harper and a British Columbia outfit came up the Liard and over the Divide; but though they found "prospects" almost everywhere in the Yukon, they did not make a real strike, so they floated to the mouth of the Yukon and went to work for the Alaska Commercial Company.

Hugh thus told the history of Yukon—so far as the white man knows it.

Although the ice still clung along the river banks, the land was free of snow, and vegetable life was asserting itself. The mosquito was very little behind the grass-shoot in realizing that summer was at hand, and that it had but a few short months in which to play its part!

It was because sleep on shore would be difficult, through the mosquitoes, that Hugh suggested their continuing the journey through the night. One watched and steered while the others slept. So Hugh, George, and Frank divided the night between them. John asserted that the rest and change of scene had done him a world of good and that he was able to steer; but the others squashed his proposals.

"Heap dam dood! heap sick all same baby, he! he!" sniggered Frank Corte.

They had now dropped away from the great mountains, not a snow-topped peak was in sight; but the hills stretched majestically on either side of the river.

The routine of watches having been decided, the party settled down to silence at nine o'clock. Towards midnight John awoke. It was now merging upon the season of perpetual light, and the hills and the great river were weirdly visible. George was on watch, sitting on the thwart ahead of him, his back towards him.

The boat quietly, swiftly glided on. No effort was needed from the man at the look-out, save an occasional stroke to keep the head straight. John glanced at his watch and saw the hour. The fact startled him, though he had schooled himself. In the lands where his previous existence had been passed the haunts of men were always at this hour illuminated by artificial light and filled with—artificiality! Here was the opening of the months-long day; and reality—Reality, the Eternal Verities. In that wonderful silence he needs must think, and overhaul his spiritual condition. He could—and he would—take Holy Orders. He would first fight the issue in the goldfields, for, if he made money, that power would be useful. So he came to his decision; and at last he slept.

When he awoke the boat was hauled half-way up one of the Yukon's many islands, and breakfast was being cooked. The party had travelled one hundred miles in twenty-four hours; three days more would carry them to Dawson.

They re-embarked, and, as the same glorious weather prevailed, their expedition was very like a delightful picnic. In the regions of Tantalus Buttes the river took a number of great horseshoe bends, which induced Hugh to remark, "We do a lot of travelling here, without much progress."

Then came Five Finger Rapids, where four great pillars of conglomerate rock stood ranged across the river. The Yukon's waters were low; the season of freshets was not due until the snow in the mountains was melted and the sun had attacked the glaciers; so Hugh said the main or right-hand channel might be run.

"Run her right on the top of the crest," he ordered.

They approached the rapid, and the current slackened almost to dead water. They rowed the boat under the cliff to the right of the channel, and then shot out into the middle, directly on the crest. The current caught the little craft—there was a swish and swirl of water—she heaved, and was over the cataract into the dancing waters beyond.

The current remained swifter than it had been above the rapids, and the party was soon at Rink Rapids, four miles beyond Five Fingers. This rapid was more dangerous than that of the Five Fingers had been, owing to its being spread over a wide range of bottom and to the presence of numerous boulders: however, they shot the boat under the right bank and glided through in safety. There now remained uninterrupted, smooth water to Dawson.

They breakfasted at Fort Selkirk, situate on the left bank of the river, opposite the mouth of the large tributary, the Pelly.

Frank protested that a day's rest would do the party good, particularly a dance that night, for there was a squaws' camp near.

"You will get all the dancing you have money to pay for in Dawson," said Hugh.

As the party were again afloat, Hugh pointed across the river, and remarked,

"Back at that bunch of bush are the ruins of old Fort Selkirk, which Robert Campbell built for the Hudson Bay Company in the year 1849. In 1852 the Chilkats burned it down, because it was cutting off their trade with the savages hereabouts. You see, before the Hudson Bay fellows got in here, the Chilkats, who held the passes to the sea, used to give inside Indians most nothing for their furs, and sell them at a big profit to the white traders on the coast. The Chilkats would not let the inside Indians out to the coast to trade for themselves. Well, when the Hudson Bay Company showed up, it broke up the cinch the Chilkats thought their own, and they came after the Company. The Indians then hereabouts, the wood Indians, got hold of the plans of the Chilkats and kept watch; but they let up for a few days, and the Chilkats came into the Fort and told the officers they had to get. It was a ground-hog case, so they just naturally got! Campbell found the local Indians and came back; but the Chilkats had cleaned out. The tea, tobacco, and sugar they took away with them, and what they couldn't take they cached. The Chilkats didn't offer to do murder, though they are up to most anything. One thing they took away with them was the Company's flag, which the Chilkats keep at Kluckwan, their village on the Chilkat River which lies in the valley just over the mountains west of Skagway. The Chilkats are very proud of their 'King George man' flag!

"It was on August 21 the Fort was seized, so Campbell had to do something right away quick, before the winter set in: so, after going down the Yukon to White River, where he met the remainder of his men, who had been to Fort Yukon and were coming back, he told them to go back down the river and winter at Fort Yukon, and he lit out up the Pelly and over the

Divide to the Liard, and down the Liard to Fort Simpson. When he got there the Liard was running bank full of ice."

The next place that drew reminiscences from Hugh was the mouth of Stewart River. Here was a police-post with a few cabins.

"In 1885, thirty miles up the Stewart, the first considerable bar diggings was struck. Dick Popham was up there in 1884, but he did not find anything—water was too high. Frank Densmore and Johnnie Hughes brought to Juneau, in the fall of 1885, the news of good gold on the Stewart; and in 1886 the gang went in, about three hundred. Along with the gang went George Carmack, but he took up with the Siwashes on the Chilkoot. You see, when the fellows started in first, the Siwashes packed from what is now Dyea to Lindeman for nine cents a pound; but as the boys were in a hurry prices rose to thirty cents—and this was too much for Carmack, who was a Missourian; besides, he got stuck on a squaw. I guess he must have stayed with the Siwashes ever since, travelling among them and living their life till he made the big strike on Bonanza, which started this here stampede.

"When the boys got to the Stewart diggings, in 1886, they found them good all right, but not enough to go round; so a lot of them lit out down the river, away below Fort Yukon, to try some prospects reported from there. Among the bunch was Bill Hartz—'Web-foot' the boys called him, because he came from Oregon. Well, those boys tried the lower diggings, and found them no good; so Web-foot started back up the river on Jack McQuestion's steamer called the *New Racket*. Jack McQuestion was trading in the country then, with Arthur Harper and Al Mayo as partners. He was in the country before Harper, and used to work for the Hudson Bay Company on the Mackenzie. At this time they had four posts—one at Fort Selkirk, one at Stewart River, one just below Dawson, and one about where Eagle City now is. There was a big mountain there called by Harper Teetotalim.

"At Teetotalim there was a queer sort of fellow from back east in Canada, a Frenchman, who was always fooling round with bits of rock, and talking about how the mountains were made. One day a Siwash blew in with a piece of woolly rock which the Frenchman said was 'Asiebestos,' and, if there was much of it, it would be worth money; so McQuestion sent out Web-foot with a grub-stake to find the place. Web-foot did not find the 'Asiebestos,' but he found gold on the Forty Mile, as also did Howard Franklin, who was sent up the Forty Mile from its mouth by McQuestion. They came back out, and on up the Yukon to winter at Stewart. Next year the fellows left Stewart for the Forty Mile, and George Matlock, Billy Leak, Oscar Ashley, and Percy Walker found Matlock Bar, with coarse gold, which washed down out of Franklin Gulch. Franklin Gulch was found in August,

1887. This was the first really coarse gold found in the Yukon, and the best discovery up to that time.

"While the boys were wintering at Stewart grub got short, and Harper passed it round, fair and square—not raising the price any. But one day some stuff was stole, and Harper told the boys, who called a miners' meeting right off. The boys appointed a committee to go round and search the cabins, for every fellow was glad enough to clear himself by showing everything he had. Nothing was found. And then the boys thought of two fellows, Missouri Bill and Arkansaw Frank, who lived down the river a bit. And when they struck a fresh trail leading to and from their cabin, they became mighty interested; and when they saw where they had made a fire, and found half-burnt-up staves of a butter firkin, they got real hot. When they got up to the cabin the door opened and the two fellows came out; one of them, Missouri Bill, with a Winchester in his hands, swearing he would shoot the first man who came a step further. This stopped the boys for a bit; but Frank Morphet got a rope off a sleigh and slipped round back of the cabin. The first thing Missouri Bill knew he had a rope round his neck—and the game was up! Well, the boys didn't want to hang them, so each of the fellows gave them a handful of beans, or a little rice, and told them to get, thinking that mushing out five hundred miles, and breaking trail all the way, was pretty nearly as bad as hanging. They made the trip all right, but it was only because they met some Siwashes."

CHAPTER XVII
DAWSON

Being in the vanguard of the multitude, whose rush to the diggings in the following year was the outstanding feature of the history of the Klondike, the Dawson that John Berwick and his companions found was that of the winter of '97, very different from the city of five thousand tents it was to become two months after their arrival!

An hour before midnight, when they arrived, Hugh had pointed out a high hill, Dawson's Dome, placed beyond the mouth of the Klondike River, or, as it was called before usage corrupted its name, the Thron Duik. Little did he or his companions dream of the part this Dome was to play in the events yet to be! The Dome was to become historic.

The main portion of Dawson was built on the north side of the Klondike. It was a scene of much movement and business. Pack-trains were passing up and down the streets, and innumerable dogs seemed everywhere.

Few boats had yet arrived, and a group of loafers gathered to watch them land. One fellow shouted, "I'll give you a dollar apiece for any late papers you have!"

Now that they were at the Klondike capital, the natural impulse of the party was to enjoy whatever amusements were available; so, in spite of their being tired, and the hour late, they drew the boat upon the gravel shore. Passing between tents, they came to the mire of the main thoroughfare. The atmosphere and circumstance of the goldfields were all about them. There were pack-horses and pack-mules waiting before the shops. Men were hurrying in and out with pack-straps on their backs. Even the dogs wore saddle-bags—a good dog being able to pack forty pounds of supplies. Other dogs passed drawing a cart, on which were half-a-dozen cans, oil-tins filled with water, dispensed at twenty-five cents the tin.

The festive side of life was more marked than the commercial. Men in wild attire, women in gorgeous raiment, were ever passing in and out of the saloons and gambling-halls. The four adventurers floundered across the mud and entered the hospitable doors of the Borealis. This was a saloon and dance-hall combined; but a roulette-wheel and faro lay-out invited to play.

It was the interval between the dances when they entered, and a loud voice was calling: "Come along, gentlemen, pretty ladies here!—just in over the ice. The next dance will be a waltz."

Frank Corte—ever the squire of dames—made a dive for the rear of the hall, and was soon leading one of the gorgeous creatures into the dizzy whirl. The partners from the last dance were crowding the bar, ordering drinks. As each man paid his two dollars his "lady" was handed a check. This check was redeemable for one dollar—the girls' source of revenue!

The orchestra was good, but the male section of the dancers was certainly grotesque; many of the men, with sombreros on their head and cigars between their teeth, were floundering through the dance in a half-intoxicated condition, their great hob-nailed boots almost drowning the music with their noise.

The three others soon left Frank to his diversions, and passed out to the street. They saw a policeman, with whom, in the way of such a free-and-easy community, they fell into talk.

"What's the chance of getting a claim?" they asked.

"Don't know. They are having stampedes right along, and any time you may hear of good pay being located on a creek. When news like this gets out there is a big rush by all classes, and you're lucky if you get anywhere near discovery. If you want work, they are paying ten dollars per day and board on the creeks for shovelling in—so I guess you need not starve!"

Hugh, with his mind on the immediate necessities of the party, asked, "Where is a good place to locate?"

"Up on the bench on the north side of the Klondike over there." The policeman pointed south-east. "You can get wood handy, and the water is good."

"What's the matter with pitching our tent where we landed?"

"Among the outfit along the water-front? No, they are the sore heads and general kickers. You don't want to tie to them. Most of them have lived in these tents all winter, and had nothing to do but dream of what some other fellow has done them out of, and how much better things would be if they had struck it rich instead of McDonald or Carmack! No, you fellows pole up-stream to-morrow to the Klondike, and then up that stream half a mile. Pack your grub to the top of the hill there, where you can live like white men."

"That sounds reasonable, but we want to sleep now."

"Well, go to Flanagan's bunk-house up the street," and the man pointed up a turning running at right angles to the main street. "He will give you beds at a dollar each."

"Our boat and things will be all right? Good-night—and thanks."

When the three visited the boat next morning they found a man standing on the bank, his legs—encased in rubber boots coming up to his hips—far apart, hands in the pockets of his overalls, a sombrero on the back of his head. Hugh noticed the smile of good-natured cynicism on his face as he regarded the boat, and said,

"Queer, ain't it? And they say there are thousands more coming."

"Yes, fifty thousand more coming in—and me waiting for a chance to get out!"

"I wonder what makes them do it?"

"Same thing as made me do it."

"Didn't you git a chance to stake anything?"

"Stake anything!—how long have you been in the country? Say! is that your boat?"

"Yes."

"Well, take my tip and just get in it, and keep right on going till you strike St. Michael's."

"For what reason would we do that?"

"Don't you know they have a Government in this country? Well, that's the reason: officials and graft! Stake a claim, and they rob you of it! No, sir, no more British mining-camps for me. I'm for the good old State of Washington. If this camp was in Alaska a fellow could hold down what was his with a shot-gun; but here you daren't make a break. Law and order!— hell! Grafters appointed by the law, and the law to see no fellow interfere with the grafters! We'd shoot the whole bunch if we had them on the other side."

"We intend to stake claims, and we intend to hold them."

"You do, eh?—well, I bet you won't. You fellows should have brought your nurse-girls with you to teach you the A B C."

The party was then joined by Frank, the habitual smile on his face; but his eyes were heavy.

"Cost me fifty dollars!" he said.

The Great Gold Rush | 95

"You got off easy—better get in and cook breakfast to wake you up. We haven't eaten yet, and meals up town cost two dollars and a half!"

"Say! if you fellows want to you can use my tent and things, but I have no grub to give away."

This invitation from the new-found pessimist was accepted, and Frank went to work cooking while their host let loose his opinions upon life.

He told them how the manager of a great trading company had the autumn before addressed the crowd, prophesying famine through the winter and exhorting all to leave the place by the only avenue of escape—the river, then filling with ice. It was a dismal picture enough, but happily worse than the reality. He spoke well of the police, and praised the way they had rushed the mail in and out with dog-teams. "And it ain't their fault there is so much grafting; they don't graft themselves."

He told of the fabulous wealth of Eldorado, Bonanza, and Hunker Creeks, and of Alec McDonald, the "Big Moose," estimated to be worth $26,000,000. He expatiated at length upon the irregularities of the Gold Commissioner's office; the iniquitous Orders-in-Council from Ottawa, such as the imposition of ten per cent. royalty on the production of the creeks, and the reserving to the Crown of every alternate claim on Dominion Creek, of all other creeks on which new discoveries might have been made, and of the hillside claims.

Frank, with his Yankee predilections, was ready to believe anything bad of Canada, and chuckled at the account. John and George, though they had had experience of official corruption in Australia, thought the accounts fantastic, and could not believe such things possible in British dominions. "The Gold Commissioner is not in the graft; he's honest—but he's like a baby, and the gang play with him as they like."

Breakfast over, the party set out, and in an hour had poled and tracked the boat half a mile up the Klondike. They passed under a crude suspension bridge and saw two ferries and innumerable boats plying across the river.

Hugh noticed a break or "draw" in the cliff, marked by a trail that led to the bench on which the party was to locate, and stopped the boat.

"Get out the axes, fellows; and, Frank, you pack the tent up the hill. It will make you think of what you have done with your last winter's wages. John, you're the honoured guest—you're going to boss the job."

Berwick, without any load, found the climb to the top of the hill sufficiently exhausting, as he was not yet fully recovered. After Frank had thrown down the tent Hugh unlashed it, and spread it in the sun, folded one end to make a pillow, and told John to lie upon it. And then he addressed his partners,

"Look here, fellows—one thing is certain. Whatever we do as regards prospecting and taking up claims, we want a home-camp as a sort of headquarters; and we might as well make it here and now. We reed not bother building a cabin, but we can put up a wall of logs the size of the tent and put the tent on top. This will do till the fall, by which time we will all be millionaires—except Frank here, unless he quits dancing! Now we'll pack up the rest of the outfit. Come on, boys!"

By four o'clock their new habitation was completed: two beds were built and the little stove erected inside the tent. Frank had an early supper and went to bed. The others built a camp-fire outside to keep away the flies, and discussed mining far into the night.

CHAPTER XVIII
POO-BAH!

During the days of his convalescence John Berwick spent many hours roaming about the bluff, indulging his passion for the sights of Nature, and thinking—quite without panic now—of the infinite problems associated with human existence in an universe governed by an inscrutable Providence. Much of his thought, too, naturally turned to the girl he had left behind him. His illness and these after-thoughts had taught him lessons, and given him hopes.

In the steep ascent, one day, of the bench on the south side of the Klondike, John came up with a tottering figure bent under a heavy load. The man was old, and the temptation came to John—invalid as he was—to offer to relieve him of the burden for a bit; when the man sat down to rest, and wiped away the perspiration with a much-soiled red handkerchief. John sat down near him; but for a time he paid no attention to him, or to any of the passers-by.

"It's a nice day," John began.

"It's only chechachoes that talk about the weather," was the blunt reply.

"I'm a chechacho."

"Don't have to tell me that: what in hell are you fellows coming here for?"

"To stake a claim and get rich."

"Poo-Bah will get it!"

"Poo-Bah—Poo-Bah of the *Mikado*?"

"This ain't the Mikie-do's Poo-Bah—this is the Octopus' Poo-Bah! He's got the Mikie-do and the Czar of Russia skinned to death. Poo-Bah comes pretty near running things in Dawson. If you stake a claim, and go to Poo-Bah and give him half interest, you may get a grant for it—that is, if Poo-Bah can't find any person to run it for him! Then, again, he may think he wants it all himself—in which case you can go to hell! If you wants to start manufacturing hootch, just go to Poo-Bah, and he will fix things so as you won't be touched."

"But are you sure? This is British territory."

"British!—nothing: this is the Octopus' country; and him and Poo-Bah is old friends! Fellows tell me Poo-Bah helped elect the Octopus back east to Parliament—or whatever you Britishers call your Government lay-out. Look at this royalty they are putting on our gold!—how much of this here royalty ever gets to Queen Victoria? No, sir; I bet Sir Wilfrid Laurier never gets his hands on one-half of what's robbed from us poor devils."

"But the expenses of Government must be raised, and you must admit that you have good law and order, and that you never get held up."

"Held up! Law and order! Hell! What's the difference between being held up by fellows like the Soapy Smith gang, or being held up by the blooming yellow-legs? You have some chance of getting clear of Soapy Smith—and it's only a matter of time till some fellow takes a shot at him; but you can't get past the yellow-legs: they won't stand for no bluffs."

"The Government will build roads."

"Roads! Then why ain't they building them? No; the Government says Poo-Bah will build them, and has given Poo-Bah a franchise to charge fellows going up Bonanza Creek trail twenty-five cents apiece, and for each pack-animal two dollars and a half. Poo-Bah started to build the road all right; but he quit just as soon as he got the toll-gate up! What do you think I'm climbing this two thousand feet for?—mountain scenery, same as you're doing? No, it's a mighty sight easier to climb this blooming hill than to wade through Poo-Bah's bog-holes. The Bonanza trail makes 'the slough of despond' look like the rocky road to Dublin! But say! I must be getting. You're away from the land of dooks and earls, and kings and queens, and all that brand of cattle; and you'd better turn white man with a new set of notions in your head."

"Let me carry your load a little way."

"Go on! I ain't dead yet! It serves me right for getting caught in a country ruled by a Government my fathers bled to get rid of, about the time of the Boston tea-party." The old man struggled into his harness again. "God! I wished I was back again under Old Glory."

John shrank under the insult. Tears came to his eyes. What soul cherishing the honour of British institutions would not have protested at such a state of things as his eyes were daily being opened to?

Sadness came over him. Here was a great injustice, and sordid, festering corruption, inspired by greed. He gritted his teeth—and a resolve came to him. If he found these stories true he would strive, somehow, anyhow, to overthrow Poo-Bah and his *clique* of corruption.

After a while John again came up to the old man resting by the side of the trail, who blurted out, "I thought I had given you enough to send you out of the country!"

"Then you didn't. Tell me this, are you aware of any case of a miner being cheated out of his claim?"

"Yes, lots. There's my own, for one."

"Where and how was that?"

The old man was not disinclined to talk.

"Well, stranger, it was this way. Me and my partner staked a claim on French Hill, and we was sure first on the ground. We went to Dawson and gave a lawyer a hundred dollars to apply for the claim for us. They told him that we must have a survey before they would give the grant. Well, we gave a surveyor two hundred dollars to survey the claim for us, and we went out there with him. When we got there with the surveyor we found a dozen fellows with rockers taking the rich pay off the rim rock. It was three weeks before we got our grant. The Gold Commissioner's gang took $30,000 out of it, and now we have the leavings, not worth much! If we hadn't thought of getting the lawyer, we wouldn't have even got the leavings!"

That was enough for John. He arose and pushed through the bushes on the opposite side of the trail, walking in the general direction of the hill-top. He desired solitude that he might think.

He felt fiercely angry at these wrongs. They were intolerable; they struck at the simplest principles of human liberty. Here were men enduring privations which sometimes caused permanent bodily harm—John remembered the snow-blinded traveller of Cape Le Berge—only to have the fruits of their strenuous endeavour mercilessly taken from them!

Before he could control his indignation he had wandered miles from Dawson, and gained the summit of the hill, where he sat to eat his luncheon.

To the eastward was the valley of the great gold-bearing creek, Bonanza. He noted the great rounded ridges, which, with their intervening valleys, ran along the slopes to its bottom. He marvelled at the softness and beauty of their lines, each of which ended in a gracefully-rounded head, standing sentinel over the creek. And well they might appear to guard its riches, for those heads contained immense deposits of bench gravels that were to cause extraordinary sensation in the days to come.

Finishing his lunch, he was idly working at the moss with his heels when he noticed that the rock beneath was white as milk. He examined it closely; yes, it was quartz, the parent rock of gold.

Immediately the instinct of the miner was aroused. He took a piece of loose rock and easily broke off several pieces. These he put into his pockets, and set out eagerly for home. His mind was free of politics now! A tinge of palest green was on the hills; this one day's sun had burst a myriad of buds upon a million poplars. Yes, it was summer!

George and Hugh, coming in soon after John's return, were shown the find, and all was enthusiasm.

"Pretty hungry-looking stuff," was Hugh's comment on close inspection. "How will you get water up there for your stamp-mill?"

John found an answer, as he remembered the long, gently-reclining ridge to Bonanza Creek with its flanking valleys on either side.

"I'll take my ore to Bonanza Creek."

"But they won't let you take the water out of Bonanza Creek."

"Perhaps not; but they will let me have the water out of the tributaries if I can turn it back before it reaches Bonanza Creek."

On the morrow George and he visited the famous—or infamous—seat of the Head over the mining industry. They found the Gold Commissioner's office a log building of no great dimensions near the police-barracks. A waiting crowd was lined before the door. A policeman standing near the office entrance directed John, who wished merely to get a copy of the regulations governing the taking up of quartz claims, to ask at the wicket inside.

He entered. As he stood waiting his turn he overheard a miner, evidently a Scandinavian, applying for a claim.

"This claim is already applied for," said the official.

"But, mister, there vos not a stake on it ven I staked it."

"I don't care! It is applied for. Next!"

"Can't I see the Commissioner?"

"No; he's busy. Next!"

"Say! mister, this is my claim."

"Next!"

Poor Ole was shoved aside by the crowd. He had waited through the weary night to gain a hearing, and now ethereal castles came toppling down!

As soon as John had obtained a copy of the regulations he and George Bruce set off to the hill of promise, each to take up a quartz claim.

They staked their claims, and then followed the ridge down to Bonanza Creek. They found that the rounded end of the ridge overlooking the creek was admirably suited as the site of a quartz mill.

"George," said his companion, "I don't think my right will be of any other use to me. I shall take up a claim here under the placer laws, and I think you had better do the same." So each of them staked a placer claim.

Instead of returning by the way they had come, the inclination to return by the creek trail was too strong to be resisted. They would be forced to wade through numerous bog-holes; but what of that? Down the hill they scrambled, and came to a sudden halt amid the full activity of some mining operations. A gang of men were working over a line of sluice-boxes, with a big fellow, standing on a pile of rocks, superintending. The water was shut off from running through the sluices. The men had lifted the riffles out of the dump-box, and the gleam of nuggets and dust was plainly visible.

"It looks good."

"It ought to be, after three days' shovelling in on discovery," answered the superintendent, who flashed a keen glance at the new-comers.

"Is this discovery?"

"That's what I endeavoured to enunciate."

"Do you object to our watching the clean-up?"

"Not that I knows of. I s'pose the gold ain't going to evaporate 'cause you look at it. But where do you come from? Are you miners?"

"We are."

"Do you want a job? Give you ten dollars and board."

"No, we have just staked claims—quartz claims on the ridge up there—and intend working them."

"Quartz! this country is full of quartz. There ain't nothing in it; see all the quartz in the wash here?" and the foreman pointed to the white pebbles among the rocks on which he was standing. "You can crack these all day and never find a colour."

"Where does the gold come from if it does not come from the quartz?"

"Where does it come from?—just grows, I guess. Gold is like potatoes in this country. It was over there, just under the bluff, that Carmack made discovery. He found a bunch of high-grade pay in the creek bottom and worked it out; and then he had to go twenty feet through the muck to bed-rock before he got the real thing. Now, how did the gold get on top of the muck where Carmack first found it? There has not been a good-sized colour found above bed-rock on any other claim on the creek. I tell you if you try to figure where gold in this country comes from, you'll go bughouse before you find out. Gold is where you find it. It's a blooming conundrum. Take me; I came up here and could have staked in on Eldorado. Well, I couldn't find a colour in the creek; but what I could see was a sign stuck up readin', 'This creek is reserved for Swedes and Moose.' Now, I weren't a Swede, and I sure weren't a Moose! So I passes her up. What happens? Why, a lot of fools take her up and she's the richest ground in the country. Nice, ain't it!—and me working for wages?"

"Well, how do you know I won't strike it rich on my quartz claim?"

"You may, stranger, you may; I've given up calling people fools for having different notions from me. Hope you will!"

They found the trail as bad as it had been described to them. It did indeed make the "slough of despond" look like the rocky road to Dublin.

Few men they met but had some humorous remark to make; and there is probably no toil greater than wading, with pack on back, from stump to stone, from stone to stump, in the course of that desperate journey. Humour was the saving grace; it was an effective barrier against despair. Occasionally men were met, blaspheming, cursing the land, the gold, the Government, but generally it was humour which made the path passable.

A led horse waded into a bog-hole. He stopped, and seemed to hesitate. "Throw a stick at him," shouted the man leading him to another who walked behind. A stick was thrown. The horse plunged, and the bog being deeper than the men had imagined, was more in the mire. "Keep him going, it's the only way to save him," was shouted. Stick after stick was hurled at the struggling animal, which became more and more bemired. It gave up the struggle. The report of a rifle soon after told that the horse was dead.

CHAPTER XIX
GRAFT

John and his fellow prospector were working with hammer and drill on their quartz claims, three weeks after they had staked them, when Hugh Spencer and Corte paid them a first visit. Hugh scrutinized the quartz his friends had mined.

"Well, this is poverty rock, for sure; why don't you quit it?"

"That's what we've been thinking lately," George confessed; "but what shall we do—go to work for wages?"

"Better earn ten dollars a day than get nothing here after blowing in your money buying grub and powder; but why not take a chance in the new stampede to Australia Creek, that runs into Dominion Creek on the Indian River side of the Divide? That's what we hunted you up for."

John and George gazed at one another. Not a word was said. John walked to the tent and began taking it down. Four packs were made of the camp and the equipment, and the party, well-loaded, returned to Dawson. So John passed from a place of many dreams.

Hugh had already made his plans.

"Australia Creek is already taken up," he said, "and, besides, it is too far away. It's two days' trip out there, about sixty miles. My idea is to hunt up a creek for ourselves. I hear the grafters in the Gold Commissioner's office already refuse applications on the grounds that the creek is all applied for. There was some sort of a row in the office when the discoverers came in to record. Things is getting pretty bad when even a discoverer is refused a record!"

"He, he! it's about time for Uncle Sam to come along," chaffed Frank, exploiting once more his set theory.

The party reached the home-camp, deposited their loads, and passed on into the town to make purchases for their projected trip. As they passed up the main street they saw a crowd collected, yelling itself hoarse. Revolvers were being fired in the air, and a frenzy of passion seemed to govern a number of individuals. A man, wild of eye, and with a disordered beard, came running down the street.

" ... man Dooey (Dewey) has knocked hell out of the Spaniards at Manilla!" he shouted.

Frank gave a cock-crow, and was off at a dive into the crowd, where a man, standing on a pile of lumber, was reading a newspaper. He would read a line, then yell and wave the paper over his head. He would again and again return to the headlines and shout them out. "Biggest sea battle since Trafalgar!"—yells—cheers—revolver shots!—"Dooey ranks with Nelson!"—more uproar!—"Rebels cut the cables, but the *Eye-Opener* gets account by special dispatch boat!"

When exhaustion had overtaken the first reader another took his place, till the owner of the newspaper was inspired to claim it and cry,

"To the Pioneer Hall, boys, and hear the full account of the biggest sea fight that was ever pulled off!—admission only one dollar."

It is said that the celebration of Admiral Dewey's victory at Manilla caused the dogs in Dawson, numbering many thousands, to leave for the hills and stay there for the space of three days!

Having bought the supplies, the next problem before the companions was to find Frank. They entered the Borealis: he was not there. Hugh suggested that his two companions should wait in the saloon while he sought the truant in other places of revelry. They remained, glad to sit, watch, and smoke, in the shaded comfort of a curtained recess.

Presently a man of giant heavy figure, with face coarse and brutal in every line, stalked into the motley crowd. His massive forehead suggested a power of brain; while his lower face showed the lines of a masterful spirit. A part of his left ear was missing; and, from the size and shape of the cut, one could readily believe the popular legend that this disfigurement had been gained in a camp brawl, and was caused by another man's teeth! To complete this awesome personality, there was a cast in one eye.

A whisper went through the crowd—"Poo-Bah!"

This, then, was the prince of grafters, the all-powerful of that region. As Poo-Bah walked towards the dancers every eye was on him; and if any face denoted anything save disgust and loathing, it was fear. A girl slid up to him and said, in a tone of confident familiarity, "Hullo! Poo-Bah. How's my baby to-night?"

"I told you not to call me that!" he answered fiercely.

"What—baby?"

"No, Poo-Bah!"

"That's what they call you," she said with a strange affectation of simplicity.

"Well, they won't make friends with me by doing so," he boomed, "and I'm a pretty good friend to have."

"Ain't you going to buy the wine?"

"I suppose so; but ain't you got that thirst of yours wet up yet?"

"I've got to live."

Just then Poo-Bah and the girl, popularly known as "Round-Eyes," were joined by two men. One was a strong big fellow with a bronzed face, who had been a master-mariner. The other was Hardman, the record clerk of the Gold Commissioner's office, evil-looking and a weakling. His small black eyes were watery.

"Hullo, fellows! The lady has suggested wine. Will you help us clean up a bottle or two?"

"Sure thing!" replied the "Cap."

Hardman was glad to agree. His eyes were watching the face of his lord, with the same expression as shines in the eyes of a hungry cur watching his master feast. Both the Cap and he had tales of woe to tell: their troubles lay sore upon them.

The party entered the booth against which John and George were sitting. As they entered and seated themselves, the two friends could hear their voices through the hangings. At first there was nothing in the words they spoke that their brazen natures would not have willingly advanced to all the world—at least, to all Dawson's world; but later the wine made them forget. They had not realized that the wall of their compartment was only a blanket.

"Two bottles of wine!" Poo-Bah demanded. The waiter brought the bottles and glasses, and Poo-Bah signed the "tab."

"Now you pay that tab, or I don't get no percentage," said the girl.

"Suppose I don't pay," answered he: "you know these damn fools from the creeks will buy all kinds of wine just to have the honour of drinking with my girl—ain't that right?"

"I guess it is," she answered, with a cold unpleasant laugh. "Because men are fools makes life easy for you and me—ain't that right?"

"Look here, I've got a kick coming," said the mariner, thumping his knee with a fist like mahogany.

"What's the matter, Cap?"

"I wrote the doctor to get me appointed as Collector of Royalty."

"You did, sure; and I backed you up: but I heard you got your appointment in the mail that got in to-day."

"Sure thing, I did."

"Well—what are you growling about? You don't want to be told how to make a dollar or two on a job like that!"

"It's going all wrong."

"What's the trouble?"

"I went down to see Smoothbore" (Smoothbore was the nickname of the head of the police), "and told him I had orders for him to put me on collecting. I guess I may have looked a little bit as if I thought I owned the earth; but I sure reckoned myself on easy street as soon as I got collecting! Well, Smoothbore, he sizes me up a bit. I guess he kind of felt I knew how to take a few ounces out of a poke and make up the weight in black sand—and then he says: 'I guess I'll send you to Thistle Creek'—Thistle Creek!—hell! They won't clean up a hundred dollars in that creek this summer; and if you'll show me how I can work a graft there, I'll be obliged."

"Anyhow, two hundred and fifty dollars a month will keep you going till something better turns up."

"Two hundred and fifty dollars a month ain't even a flea-bite, seeing what it costs to live like a gentleman in Dawson. You can't eat under ten dollars a day!" His voice faded in a growl. Poo-Bah took up the running.

"The thing is, we've got to get Smoothbore relieved from command here. He puts backbone even into Hi-u Bill" (Hi-u Bill was the District Commissioner). "We've got to get a putty man."

The others agreed cordially. John and his companion, who had before felt like going, looked at each other, and silently decided to stay.

"What kick have you got, Hardie?" they heard Poo-Bah ask.

"Kick!" whined the little man. "I've got lots of kick. We had a row in the office to-day."

"I heard something of that. What was the row?"

"Some Australians came in." John and George looked at each other and grimly smiled. "I sized it up that they had staked something rich. I tried to tell them that the creek they wanted to record on was all taken up—intending, of course, to put you in on discovery."

"Yes, yes."

"Well—the cockneys just pulled five guns and said, 'Record those claims.' I made a break as if to get the books, intending to get out the back door; but the old man comes out of his office and catches on. He turns white around the gills, and says, 'Record those claims.' Of course, I just had to give record!"

"But where does Smoothbore come in?"

"He comes in all right. I'm just from him now. I went down after supper to see him to find out if an example could not be made of the cockneys—thinking if we got them on the wood-pile[9] we would have a chance at their claims after all. He was alone, walking up and down the mess. 'Sit down,' he says, and I sits. 'What is it?' I had to tell him the story straight. You see, he is a hard man to lie to, and I knew he already had the story. After I got down to telling him of the old man ordering me to record the claims, he says, 'And you recorded them?' 'Yes,' says I. 'The men did not ask you for any money?' 'No.' 'In fact, they only desired to assist your memory to the point that you had never before recorded the claims they asked for?' 'I guess so,' says I. 'This is what you must say if you give evidence against them.' And then I thinks a bit, and I says, 'You couldn't give them twenty-four hours to get out of the country, could you?' 'No,' says he; 'if I do anything I arrest them and bring them to trial, which I will do as soon as you swear out information.' 'I guess I won't do that,' I says. Now, look here, Poo-B——, oh, all right, Smoothbore ain't with us, he's against us, and it's up to you to get him fired." Hardman had ended his long speech.

[9] In jail.

"It might not be easy," said the heavy man thoughtfully.

"Yes, it will; Laurier will do anything our boss says these days: you fix it!"

"That's right," the Cap put in. "Hardie's right again!"

"You'd be a long time in Nova Scotia before you'd earn two hundred and fifty dollars a month! Eh, Cap?" sneered the girl.

"Earn! How much do you earn here? You graft same as the rest of us."

"Quit fighting," Poo-Bah broke in, and their querulous voices ceased. "Cap, I think I see how you can make a dollar or two: and you'll be near our friend, Hardie, here; besides being in a position to pick up information for the benefit of yours truly. I'll see the Gold Commissioner, and get you put on as special door-keeper instead of a policeman. Guess your dignity will stand up under this! You will have the right to let fellows into the office on special appointment—see?—which will cost a ten or a twenty!"

"Not so bad!" slowly muttered the Cap, while the girl gurgled her appreciation. "The thing looks to have possibilities, and I guess my dignity will stand it."

Just then Hugh, with Frank at his heels, came in.

"Wait till I have just one dance," cried Frank, and was off to the room where music was to be heard. John motioned to Hugh to be still. They listened eagerly.

"Now, I've got some news—blamed noise those people make!—came in the mail to-day," went on Poo-Bah. "Orders have come from Ottawa throwing open the hillside claims of Dominion. I won't mind you fellows getting a claim or two; but I want to get a bunch."

"You'll get hold of yours before the news is made public," suggested the Cap.

"No, that won't hardly do," drawled Poo-Bah; "you see there'll be hell enough raised when it is found I get a bunch of claims; and while Ottawa is ready enough to take our explanation of things, there is such a thing as being too coarse, even here—besides, it ain't necessary. No, in a few days the news will be made public: till then keep your heads shut, see?"

"We'll trust you to work the graft," said the girl.

"You can certainly rely on me! Now, people, I've got to pull my freight."

Hugh gripped John's arm, but he released it as he saw the party were leaving the box. The friends shrank back further into the shadows. When they were gone he whispered,

"Did you hear that? Dominion hillsides to be thrown open! Some of the richest ground in the country."

"I heard them talking about grafts, and I heard complaints about Smoothbore—who ever that may be."

"The Colonel at the Barracks."

"They appear to find him in the way." John hurriedly gave some account of what they had overheard. Hugh's eyes glistened.

"Sure thing! Smoothbore is in the way. He's straight; but this last about Dominion is the news. We'll get in on the hillsides of Dominion, and do our best to hold them."

It was late enough for rest, especially for weary workers such as they: so they passed through the streets directly for the home-camp. Dawson was now the home of twenty thousand people, ninety-nine per cent. adult males. Its streets were a wide range of strange sights and wild scenes. Its outskirts were of tents, and yet more tents.

They went to bed with the waking dreams of wealth very close to them. John Berwick, who had some qualms at taking advantage of what he had overheard, felt it was an unsatisfactory condition of things in which such a malefactor as Poo-Bah could swagger and flourish.

CHAPTER XX
A LOTTERY

On the second day after leaving Dawson, John Berwick and his partners camped on Dominion Creek, worn out and weary. Their commissariat was equal to a three weeks' stay, and their tools and their bedding were added to the load. Hugh remained their leader. While John and George had been prospecting their quartz find, he had visited Dominion Creek, and found many miners looking with avidity towards the claims on the left limit of the creek, several miles below the confluence of Caribou. It was to this locality that he directed the party.

The laws governing the taking up of placer-claims in the Yukon demanded that the applicant should swear to the finding of gold. No quantity was mentioned. John and George had met this difficulty when they applied for the placer-claims on the Bonanza hillsides; but this technicality had been smilingly dispensed with by the record clerk on the consideration that nobody wanted the ground for placer. In the case of the Dominion Creek hillsides, however, they determined to make discoveries, if possible.

They pitched their tent upon the hillside, which rose in a gentle incline from the creek. If any former channel ran underneath the ground they had chosen it could not be very far to bed-rock.

They picked their four claims, and numbered them 1, 2, 3, 4. They drew lots for them. John had 1, Hugh 2, Frank 3, and George the 4th.

As their tent was small they determined that two of them should work at night-time and two by day. This also meant that a continuous watch could be kept. Miners from the creek claims visited them, curious to learn their motive. When they were told that the party expected the claims to be some day thrown open, they smiled in superior wisdom.

Each of the four began to sink a shaft to the bed-rock of his claim. A single man can sink a hole ten, even twelve, feet: but after that a windlass is necessary to hoist the dirt.

It was arranged that the first day they all should work, George and Frank continuing the watch through the night. They began early in the morning of the first day, each on his claim. Each made a little clearing around the spot he had chosen as the locality of his first shaft. The growth was not heavy, and was quickly disposed of. By noon each had made a hole about three feet deep. No frost was met as yet.

It was George who first reached bed-rock at five-foot depth! He went to the other workers and announced the fact. Hugh had expected it to be thirty, or twenty-five, feet at least. Their first feeling was of disappointment.

The party gathered about the pit, and Hugh jumped into it. There was about a foot of gravel above the bed-rock. Hugh picked out a pebble lying directly on bed-rock, and smoothed over its muddy surface with his fingers. His eyes brightened. It gleamed with half-a-dozen specks of gold. He passed it up to the others, who gazed on it gladly. They gave him a pan. Hugh scooped it full of gravel and scrambled out of the hole. The others turned towards the creek.

"No, fellows, I've got a pool located up in the bushes here," and he looked away from the creek. "What those fellows on the creek don't know won't do them no harm." He led the way through the bushes. Arriving at the pool, he dipped the pan into the water and shook it. He then placed it on the ground, grabbed a handful of the pebbles, washed them in the water of the pan, and threw them away. He continued this process till he had removed the larger stones. Then again he whirled the pan in the water, this time more vigorously. He picked out the smaller pebbles, and replaced the pan in the water, whirled and shook it again, frequently lifting it out on an incline, allowing the off-rushing water to carry away the small pebbles and sand.

This process he kept up till but a handful of stuff remained at the bottom. He kept the pan on an incline, which caused the stuff to remain at one side. He moved the pan gently to and fro, with occasional quick shakings; very gently he drew the pan in and out of the water, the ebb to draw off the lighter sand. The residue in the pan became but a spoonful or two, and now occasionally a golden speck shone and gleamed. The sand in the pan became less, and some of it was black—the black sand of the miners, magnetic from the iron which so largely composes it. As the process proceeded the sideward motion occasionally carried the body of black sand away, leaving a trail of gleaming yellow dust. The black sand had at last all been washed over the side of the pan. Hugh, with his fingers, massed the gold into a little pile, and muttered, "Seventy-five cents."

"Three bob," George repeated after him. The pan was passed from hand to hand for scrutiny and comment.

"Not bad!" said John.

"You bet it ain't!" agreed Hugh, "even if it don't rank with Eldorado. This ground ain't deep, and the surface can be ground-sluiced off. Let us try another pan off of bed-rock."

The pan was again filled and the process of washing resumed. "If we get two cents in this gravel a foot off of bed-rock I'll be satisfied," was Hugh's comment. He got this time what he estimated to be five cents. "Perhaps this is above average," he muttered. Your old-time miner is ever a sceptic.

So while he was washing this second pan Hugh's mind was at work.

"George, I guess you had better go and chuck back all the gravel and wash into the hole and get a fire built on it quick. The ashes will hide the wash, and any person looking down the hole will simply think that you have struck frost and are using fire. The rest of us will keep going till we strike wash."

Frank reached gravel at about seven feet, and reported the same to Hugh, who suggested that he should work a small hole to bed-rock to get a pan of gravel from that point. Hugh cautioned Frank against throwing any gravel out of the shaft to attract the notice of passers-by.

Frank secured a pan of dirt immediately on bed-rock, and Hugh panned it for him. Frank was the only one of the four not a miner.

The pan yielded a little better than that of George had done. Hugh suggested, significantly, that Frank had found frost at the bottom of his shaft, which induced the latter to mutter: "Ground heap frozen all same rock, no ketchum gold without fire, he! he!" This was supposed to be a humorous imitation of the Siwash.

"Never mind your Siwash sweethearts, but get the fire in quick. I suppose if you do strike it rich, or ever get this claim, which is sure worth something, it will be heap klootch, heap dance, all the time! Get a move on, or some rubber-neck will be mooching round here!"

Hugh went back to his pit, and both he and John had struck real frost before Frank roared, "Supper!"

During the meal, and afterwards, the conversation was about the claims and the prospect of their getting them. It was two weeks yet before they could be judiciously staked. In the meantime, Frank and George could put down other shafts prospecting the width and extent of the pay streak, while John and Hugh were getting their shaft down to bed-rock. It would be slow work for these two, now that they had struck frost, which necessitated thawing by wood-fires.

"I guess we need a cabin on these claims," said Hugh. "It's more a sign we're holding them down, and if we start building it we can kill time so as not to look conspicuous, as we would if we was just to sit and do nothing. It would have the rubber-necks guessing."

So the work continued upon the four hillside claims on Dominion Creek, John and Hugh working at day, George and Frank at night. These two, holding the vigil of the second night, again found bed-rock and gold, twenty feet further up the hillside than their first shafts.

On the day following John and Hugh quickly cleared the bottom of their shafts of the earth which the fires, burning through the night, had thawed. They then set new fires, and sat in the shade of a tree while they burned. The bed-rock on each of their claims was deeper than that on the claims of their two associates, and both felt that their claims would prove the richer, though neither of them uttered this thought. The minds of all were planning how best to gain possession of their discoveries.

"I guess," said Hugh, as he lit his pipe, and slapped divers mosquitoes to death, "that it ain't altogether judicious for George and Frank to perforate this here landscape with any more shafts. There is sure to be some fellows rubber-necking here soon. I see some water has seeped into the two holes they sunk first, and the other two will probably fill soon. This will keep others from investigating. I guess they had better get to work on a cabin, which we will help them with as soon as we get bed-rock ourselves. These claims is mighty well worth holding on to, and we don't want to run no chances of not getting them—which we, sure, won't do if Poo-Bah's gang gets on to the fact that they are any good."

When the four were seated round the evening meal the matter was talked over, and Frank and George agreed to start building a cabin. The work was begun that very night.

Days came and went; yet neither John nor Hugh found bed-rock, although each shaft was now fifteen feet deep. At twelve-foot depth a windlass had been constructed on each claim, and the earth hoisted from the shaft. At eighteen feet Hugh struck gravel. As John, who worked the windlass, dumped a bucket of gravel, he would hide it by shovelling over it earth from the dump. Finding gravel there at that depth suggested gold; in fact, the depth to which the shaft was sunk without striking bed-rock was sufficiently compromising.

At last bed-rock was reached, and a pan of dirt extracted. The pan was washed, and a nugget worth fully a dollar and a half, besides about two dollars in fine gold, was its product. Here was wealth and no mistake!

"Hi-u chickaman stuff, he! he!" laughed Frank. They all looked into each other's eyes. Hugh gritted his teeth as he thought of Poo-Bah. If there was any extent of this gravel it constituted a fortune—yes, very little of this ground meant wealth. How much of it would there be? Was this gold of Dominion Creek pay-streak? He did not know: the great thing about mining is, you never know.

John's shaft found bed-rock at twenty-two feet, where he got a good five dollars to the pan. Frank jabbered; the others said but little.

It was late in the afternoon when the pan of dirt from John's shaft was tried. After supper Hugh took a stroll. He walked far up the hillside, and gazed at the tributary valley that ran into Dominion Creek, just up-stream from John's claim. This "pup"—as the miners term these small tributaries—Hugh noticed had been staked and prospected, but had not yielded pay. He had already planned to use its water for the washing of the gravel should he gain possession of his claim.

He then walked down to the adjacent claim being worked on Dominion Creek, and began asking questions of the man at the windlass. He was always ready to receive information, though he seldom gave any. The ground on Dominion was rich—enormously rich—ten, twenty, and sometimes fifty dollar pans. Up-stream the second claim was not nearly so rich. The man at the windlass did not know the value of the intervening claim; it was held by the Government.

"How far are you to bed-rock?"

"About twenty-five feet."

"Much gravel?"

"About three feet—hardly three feet."

Hugh was tempted to ask how deep the miners, who had prospected the pup, had gone before they had struck pay; but did not, because he gave the man credit for intelligence.

"Black muck above gravel?" he asked.

"Yes, or we would not be working with wood-fires now. Black muck takes a lot to thaw; but, as it is, I guess we shall have to quit till winter—but we have proved our ground rich."

Until the advent of steam-thawing machines, the Klondike miners thawed their ground by wood-fires, which process can only be carried on extensively in winter.

Hugh left the miner and walked to the mouth of the pup. With a pole he sounded the depth of an abandoned shaft. It was fifteen feet. He walked to the camp and found John, the others being at work on the cabin.

"John, the bed-rock at the bottom of your shaft dips towards my claim, and the bed-rock in my shaft dips towards your claim."

"Yes."

"The fellow at the windlass on the creek claim tells me that he is in the biggest kind of pay outside of Eldorado, but that the second claim upstream is not up to much. He has muck."

"Yes."

"We have earth and broken rock down to the gravel."

"Yes."

"His shaft is twenty-five feet to bed-rock, and if we sank a shaft halfway between yours and mine we would find it deeper than either."

"In all probability, yes."

"Don't you see what I am driving at?"

"No," John answered bluntly.

"You've caught on to that pup up-stream there."

"I have!"

"Well, it's only fifteen feet to bed-rock there. The old channel of that pup runs underneath your claim and mine and is mighty rich. The gold found on the creek claim looks exactly like ours: I saw some of it lying in a pan."

John was watching the face of his friend intently.

"These hillside claims are two hundred and fifty feet long, and stretch one thousand feet back, which means the chances are that the claims you and I are prospecting cover one thousand feet of mighty rich ground."

"We are wealthy men," said John.

And his thought passed in a flash to Alice Peel.

"Hold on!—we ain't got them yet," counselled Hugh.

His mind reverted to Poo-Bah.

CHAPTER XXI
THE PEELS' HOSPITAL

Alice Peel and her father, the Surgeon-Major, arrived in Dawson by one of the first steamers from St. Michael's. It was late in the evening when they docked, so they arranged to stay on board all night. This made it possible for them to see some of the sights ere they retired. They landed and mingled with the crowds preparatory to finding lodgings. Alice suggested they should ascertain the whereabouts of the Rector. Her father did so; and when he thanked the man of whom he inquired, added, "I'll look him up to-morrow."

"Might as well do so right away, quick; he's always hangin' round there."

"But it's eleven o'clock."

"Don't make no difference in Dawson."

Alice and her father, thereupon, picked their way towards the Police Barracks, where, on the banks of the "slough," rested the little log church. It was shut off from the street by a rustic fence—a peaceful sight. Alice and her father were standing regarding it, and had almost made up their minds to enter, to see if any one was about, when their attention was attracted by a man in a boat mooring his craft beside the church grounds. He landed his bundle of blankets, and was spreading them under the church window, when a slight figure with bared head stepped out of the door and stood looking at the intruder.

The man folded up his coat that it might serve as a pillow, and was placing it in the prescribed position, when the Rector spoke.

"You'll have to get out of this."

The man looked up and stared.

"Say! Parson, are you any relation to the Good Samaritan?"

This was rather a poser; a suitable reply was evidently not ready on the moment.

"No, I'm not, I'm sorry to say—but what's the matter with you?"

"Just broke! Besides, if I wasn't, I don't see why I need pay a dollar for a bed when I have my own blanket. What are you—High Church or Low Church?"

"I'm anything you like; but you'll have to get out of this. If you sleep there you'll roll over and crush my flowers. But what are you?"

"Everything you don't like, I guess."

"No, that you're not. But the thing is, if I let one of you fellows camp here, I'll have a hundred in no time."

"All right! I don't mind sleeping inside the church, if you don't want the other fellows to see me!"

What could be done with such a man?

"But I'm going to have service at twelve o'clock for any of the boys coming in from the creeks."

"I don't mind the services: singing won't keep me awake; and as for sermons!..."

"It looks as if I can't get rid of you. I suppose I'll have to stand for it! Roll up your blankets; you can sleep inside after service."

As the clergyman turned to re-enter the building he noticed Alice and her father regarding him and his guest with some amusement. He advanced to them, and held out his hand.

"We arrived this evening, and thought we should like to look you up and gain some knowledge of Dawson, and the manners and customs of its people," said Alice.

"You have evidently been enjoying an exhibition of them. Come in and see our church."

They entered the yard and walked towards the door, watching the intruder wrestle with his bedding. They passed into the church, and to Alice it seemed fitting that this should be the first log building she had ever entered, the first roof to cover her in the New World. Being a thorough Churchwoman it was to her a matter of satisfaction and sentiment.

As they stood before the altar others entered, whereupon their host looked at his watch.

"It is almost time," he said.

"May we stay?" asked Alice.

"Assuredly."

The night was cloudy outside, and the church too dark for reading, so the clergyman brought out and placed two candles upon the altar. The father and daughter each noted the candlesticks were bottles. "How incongruous!" thought the Surgeon-Major. The one had evidently held gin, the other whisky.

The service was short, just a lesson and a hymn. Only half-a-dozen were present. When it came to the hymn the clergyman beckoned to Alice and her father. Each accepted from the clerk's hand a bottle and a candle, and he motioned them to stand on either side of him. This they did, he holding the hymn-book. They sang, "I need Thee every hour."

After the service the new-comers waited for the clergyman, and the three passed down towards the door. The intruder was already making his bed.

"Say! Parson, that wasn't bad," he said.

"What wasn't bad?"

"That there tune; but I never thought you'd confess it."

"Confess what?"

"That you needed it every hour. Isn't that what you meant by having the chechachoes hold the bottles?"

"No, it wasn't!" The Parson was annoyed. "You get out of here in the morning, or I'll throw you into the slough."

"All right, Pard."

"Your friend seems somewhat facetious," remarked Surgeon-Major Peel.

"Yes, they are all friends of mine. They all know me: if they don't, their friends do. This man is a type of what I have to deal with."

Then they settled down to the business on which the Peels had called.

"If you have the necessary supplies," said the Parson, "a private hospital is the thing. There is a great deal of sickness now. The typhoid is getting bad; too many living in the manner of our friend at the church. Food poor and badly-cooked, general uncleanness; hard trails and stampedes."

The Parson conducted the new-comers to their boat, and left them satisfied and almost contented. Alice asked him, as he was taking his leave, if he knew John Berwick; but had for answer, No. She wanted to inquire at the post-office; but could not get near enough on account of the long lines of men standing before the wickets, postal affairs being in a state of chaos. It was evidently more than possible that John had not received her letters, or, at any rate, the communication which told of her coming.

On the morrow the Peels, giving fulfilment to their intentions, secured a building in Dawson; and so St. George's Private Hospital came into being.

It was a matter of much detail. Help and assistance of every kind was enormously dear. They had changed their money into gold dust, and each carried a "poke." Alice was astounded when she reckoned the equivalent of the charge made by the man who brought their heavy luggage. Half an ounce of dust meant thirty shillings. There were no idle hands in Dawson; it was the hum of industry, except with the loungers at the water front.

Alice worked hard, and her work brought distraction. Now she was near John Berwick—at least, she ought to be, but had heard of so many cases of drowning, deaths by fever and scurvy in that terrible country, that she could only fear possibilities, and eagerly scan every face she met. She stared into the faces of men of uncouth beards and matted greasy hair; and, as was the custom of the country, her gaze was returned. All seeing her, wondered what had brought this fragrant, gentle English girl to Dawson. She was so different from the women of the underworld, hitherto the only representatives with one or two exceptions of womanhood in that place. Her fresh complexion contrasted with their painted cheeks; her simple grace with their brazenness and vulgarity. "Oh, it was pitiful!"

In the shops—wherever she went—she asked about John Berwick. Only once was she in some measure successful.

"I think there was a fellow by that name bought a bill of goods and said he would be back for them later, one day, not long ago. He must be living near Dawson," said the man.

"Why do you say that?" eagerly asked Alice.

"Because the grub he bought weren't the kind of grub men takes with them on long trips; besides, he didn't buy enough to last him long."

She thanked him; and left her name and address in Dawson.

Alice was possessed of the faith that only death can kill, and that faith gave her patience. She buckled to her work, and was content. Had she been less industrious she might have found the trails up the Dome—and to John; but no sooner had the hospital opened than patients came pouring in. Nurses of experience were impossible to obtain. She and her father had to struggle with the help of only one woman and three men. All were untrained and inexperienced.

CHAPTER XXII
THE LAST STRAW

One night George ran into the tent, and shook life into John and Hugh.

"They're here!"

"Who?"

"Poo-Bah's gang."

At once the two were wide awake. Hugh stuck his head out of the tent, and saw a number of men walking down the creek carrying stakes over their shoulders. He darted back, and clambered into his clothes. John followed his example.

"Where's Frank?" asked Hugh.

George went to the tent door, and gave a low whistle. Frank made his appearance. Each man armed himself with his two stakes, and made towards the down-hill limit of his claim, and drove them in at their proper places. One stake bore the legend, "I claim 250 feet down-stream and 1,000 feet up-hill for placer-mining purposes. John Berwick, Miner's License No. T. 64859." The other was similar, except that it claimed up-stream. The claims were staked in the small hours of July 12 in the year 1898 — the day of the great Dominion Creek stampede.

The party then ate a hasty meal, and took food for luncheon. At about four o'clock they set out for Dawson, a distance of forty miles. They hoped to reach the city by 6 p.m.

They passed the minions of the great grafter.

"Travelling early, gentlemen!" said one of them.

"Not so many flies," answered Hugh.

Occasionally wild-eyed men passed them, with a stride that seemed as if it could never tire. This was an hour or two after John and his friends had set out. These men had evidently been given "the tip" the night before, and had begun to travel at once.

News spreads in a mining-camp with amazing rapidity, and the crowd of hurrying men grew greater as the party progressed. It was also noted that the fever was most marked in those who felt themselves at the rear of the stampede. Those in the lead carried nothing save a little axe—their body's sustenance was in their pockets, often consisting only of a few pots of beef extract. When time for resting came the little axe would serve to make a spruce bed. Covering was not needed in the summer, as rest was taken in daytime—often in the full glare of the sun—a form of repose generally limited to negroes and savages.

The 12th of July, 1898, was one of the hottest days of the hottest season Dawson had ever known. The thermometer was nearly ninety in the shade. The land was parched for water, and the smoke of forest-fires filled the air, which seemed to burn the throats of those mad men. They coughed as they hurried by.

The party passed the Bonanza Dome and commenced the decline into the Bonanza Valley. The trail followed the hog's-back which ends in Carmacks Forks, the confluence of two branches of the Upper Bonanza.

The descent to them was rapid, and the steep ascent of a thousand feet seemed terrible to the stampeders. Yet up it they stormed and struggled till they fell exhausted. Even in the glaring sun men lay dead beat, panting. They were twenty miles from Dawson; twenty hard miles yet rested between them and their goal!

It seemed as if this stampede were born of frenzy in a last final effort of the desperate gold-seekers of that year. They were close to the end of the rainbow, where lay prizes for a few. There was no more of the old affected humour of the road. Drawn faces and staring eyes were telling of soul-strain. It was the last scene of the last act of a real tragedy!

At the spring beneath a group of stunted spruce-trees—at which, more or less, every man who has sought the glittering dust of the Klondike has gained refreshment—the party of four halted for lunch. A dozen men were already about it in all postures of fatigue. As soon as one got up and staggered on his place was occupied by a new-comer, who would gulp his fill of the blessed water and lie for a time inert. They came and they went. Not a word was said.

"Where are you stampeding to?" John at last asked one, who seemed less exhausted than the others.

"I don't know; just following the crowd. Something doing on Dominion, they say, the hillsides. Some say the creek claims held by the Government are being thrown open, but I guess not."

Just following the crowd! It is ever the way in gold rushes. No wonder the man who had advised them to "keep on going till they struck St. Michael's" had said it was a disease!

They passed on down the Bonanza trail; soon the majority of the people met were other than the stampeders. The stampeders were in the crowd, but the bulk were those engaged in the ordinary economic development of Bonanza.

They passed from the Valley of Bonanza, after each had contributed the usual twenty-five cents to the coffers of Poo-Bah. Here they were but a mile or two from Dawson, and the flood of stampeders had passed. As they approached the ferry they noticed a group of men standing before a cabin, evidently examining something. They joined the crowd and saw a little woman with an infant in her arms.

"My! look at the baby," said an individual bearing the superior dignity of an old-timer; "it's the first white baby I've seen in six year; kind of makes me think of home. You say it was born inside here?"

"Yes, right here in this cabin, where my husband and I have wintered. He is off on the stampede."

"I've only been in the country two months, yet the sight of that baby makes me think of a land where there ain't no Bonanza Creek trail," sighed a chechacho. "Ain't you frightened to live here alone?"

"No. Nobody will harm a respectable woman in Dawson." The speaker's face shone with pride, which was not all that of motherhood.

The old-timer threw a nugget of gold on the baby's breast as he walked away, desiring that the mother should buy the child something. The contribution was becoming general, when the mother protested. She knew there were many in the crowd who could not afford such a gift, and that any miner would part with his last cent rather than appear before his fellows as lacking in generosity or holding anything but a contempt for money.

To cross Poo-Bah's ferry cost each person an additional twenty-five cents. There was none other than Poo-Bah's ferry, for his franchise was exclusive. Many impoverished prospectors had attempted to retrieve their fortunes by plying at the river, but were stopped.

After eating their evening meal at the home-camp the party passed down into the city to take their places in the line before the Gold Commissioner's office. None of the Dominion Creek stampeders had yet arrived, and the line was its usual length. They knew that ere the morning arrived the line would be much increased and hundreds would have arrived within twenty-four hours. So, as nine o'clock came, they all lay down at full length on the earth and slept, indifferent to the current of life about them. This was the life of the goldfields—absolute lack of conventionality and indifference to social distinction.

Just before John fell asleep he noticed some men slipping into the Gold Commissioner's office by a side door, among whom were Hardman and the "Cap." Mentioning this on the day following, Hugh remarked that they had stayed in the office till late.

In the morning a policeman was consulted, and Frank was commissioned to leave his place in the line, visit a shop, and buy tinned meat and biscuit. The policeman would recognize Frank when he returned and see that he got his place. So the friends secured their morning meal.

As was expected, the morning saw the arrival of the first of the Dominion Creek stampeders; they had staked their claims and returned to add to the length of the waiting line. Their faces and appearance told something of the terrors of their experience.

Bodies limp and eyes glazed, faces wan and expressionless, these were the result of thirty-six hours of intense muscular and nervous strain. The gold frenzy is the hardest, harshest, of tax-masters, drawing its victims into such self-inflicted labour as, if imposed by an employer, would rouse the protests of civilized humanity. Such toil breeds the determination to have and to hold what is justly won, develops sympathy for the rights of others, and will push aside the laws of custom and society if they stand in the way of justice.

The office doors were opened and the slow procession began. It was an hour past noon when John and his three companions stood before the wicket where the whiskered Hardman was at work. Hugh came first, John next, then George, lastly Frank.

"We want to record hillsides on Dominion," said Hugh.

"What numbers?"

"I have lower half, fifty below centre discovery, left limit, and my friend here has upper half."

Hardman grabbed a book and turned over the leaves to the space allotted these claims.

"These claims are already recorded," which answer was not unexpected.

"When were they staked?" Fatigued though he was, Hugh's face was livid with anger.

"At one minute past midnight of the 11th of July, 1898."

"No, they wasn't."

"Well, that is what the affidavit says which I entered late yesterday afternoon."

John now interposed. "We have been camped on this ground for three weeks, and have been on continuous watch. We staked these claims at 4 A.M. yesterday. No stakes were in the ground when we staked."

"I can't help that; Joseph Trudean swears he staked one, and Ole Anderson swears he staked the other."

"Say! have these claims been transferred?" asked Hugh.

"Yes, each has been sold to James C. Beecher, barrister, of Dawson."

"And the consideration?"

"One dollar."

"Which would not buy a meal in Dawson!"

Sick and beaten, John and Hugh stepped aside; George and Frank passed to the slaughter. Their friends waited for them. The time to wait was not long—the second two being even more quickly disposed of than the first.

They went home, and ate a meal. Even Frank was reduced to seriousness, his only possible return to cheerfulness being when he said, "He! he! I told you it was time Uncle Sam came and took Canada!" John Berwick felt himself prompted to say "Amen."

They early sought repose, but about nine in the evening John arose and dressed himself. He had slept but four hours when he suddenly awakened. Something called him to action. Hugh awakened too, and asked the time. He, then, also arose, as did the others. No one explained why he was dressing, or what he intended to do. Without words each knew they were going to the city—the call was on them to enter the haunts of men—to speak of their wrongs and to be heard!

They had tea, and set out over the trail called after the great Alaska Commercial Company, who built it to the city. The flowers that bloomed by the wayside drew the eyes of John, who, even in this hour of disappointment and anger, was alive to the beauties of nature. The dog-roses, great in size and delicate in colour, greeted him as old friends, and carried his mind to England and to Alice.

The atmosphere of Dawson was latent with strong emotion. There was no noise. A malamoot howled, and those hearing him shuddered. Men stood in groups and talked; their tones were low, their eyes alert. But in the Borealis Saloon Joseph Andrews jumped upon the bar and addressed the house. That he suspended the dance, which brought the proprietor many hundreds of dollars daily, was overlooked in the face of national disaster; for these men of Dawson had become as a nation—united and distinctive.

John Berwick and his friends were drawn by the voice that came through the door of Dawson's most popular rendezvous. Straining to look over the heads and shoulders in front of them, they saw a man, red in face, through the strain of his oratory, standing on the bar and gesticulating. A crowd of eager men listened to him intently.

"I tell you fellows from South Africa that the Government of this here country has got that of Paul Kruger done to a finish. Oom Paul is a genius at grafting; but where does he figure, with his coarse schemes of dynamite monopolies, in comparison with the liquor-law handed out by the gang of thugs and highway robbers who run this country? I tell you the Octopus and his liquor-permit system has got Paul Kruger beaten to death. Permit system! permit system! permit system! nothing! Graft, graft, graft! that's what it is, graft! The Octopus tells the good ladies down East that he doesn't approve of the liquor traffic; that he won't allow any liquor to go into this country unless by special permit from him! But what are these permits? They're handed out in ten thousand gallon blocks, and there's enough whisky in Dawson City, and on the way here, to float a battleship. And who gets the permits? His own pals and the Jews. Jews, gentlemen, Jews! and the *quid pro quo* is a contribution to this same Octopus's electioneering fund. Here, gentlemen, under a surface-showing of morality and pink-tea temperance, are true fissure veins of graft, assaying high in craft and subtlety. Men of the Yukon, are we going to stand for it? Have we got to stand for it? There are fifty thousand of us, gentlemen! Are we yelping coyotes or are we men?" The speaker paused, that his words might sink in. His audience answered with a yell; and then were hushed again.

"But after all, this liquor business is only a marker on the rest, only a token. Dominion Creek hillsides—Dominion Creek hillsides—is where Poo-Bah, our own Octopus's own 'Man-Friday,' has got in his fine work! Orders came from Ottawa that these claims were to be thrown open, and posters were printed and stuck up saying the time was July 14th. Then, when the twelfth came round, somebody finds a mistake was made, and the proper date is the twelfth. We rush the creek, gentlemen, and stake—what? Nothing!—we get nothing! There are fifty thousand of us, gentlemen, and every man has two rifles and a shot-gun. Are we going to stand for it?"

"No," was the general shout.

"We've all been over the Passes and we've run chances—big chances; most of us have had a handshake with death, cold grimy death! Can't we shake hands once again? Are we men, or only mangy malamoots?" He paused; but there was no cheer at this moment. They were all too eager for him to continue.

"What is our situation, gentlemen? Look at our situation! We're two thousand miles from nowhere, and those two thousand miles are mountains—snow and glaciers! Talk about Napoleon's retreat from Moscow! That was just a game of ping-pong compared to marching an army across country from back East to the Yukon! just a little lally-gag. The White Pass, and the Chilkoot Pass, and the mouth of the Yukon, belong to Uncle Sam...."

At the mention of "Uncle Sam" a great cheer went up—a mighty shout. "Uncle Sam! Hurrah for Uncle Sam! he won't tax our gold!"

"No, no, gentlemen—the Republic of the North!—a Republic of the North!—we can work out the mines before trouble can come to us," said the speaker.

"The Klondike Free State! The Klondike Free State!" shouted a man. The crowd took up the cry. Chaos reigned.

John Berwick, who had pushed his way through the crowd, sprang upon the bar beside Joseph Andrews the orator. He raised his hand for silence.

CHAPTER XXIII
REVOLUTION

"Is a man's life to be mere existence—breathing, and the eating of food with hours of repose; or is it to be striving after some ideal, whether of ambition or duty? Strife, surely! Man spends his life in toil; the results of his labour represent his life. Imagine for one moment that we are standing upon Dawson's Dome." The audience began to cough and shuffle. This exordium was unusual. The men seemed restless, and then, as if with an unanimous impulse, they appeared to settle to attention. John went on, "We turn our faces to the north and view a mass of gorgeous colouring—the shield of the day that is past and the herald of the day that is to come. To the south and east and west this beauty is reflected in blended tints, sinking into valleys purple and silent. Whence came these valleys? They mark the erosion of ages: as a day is to a thousand years, so is the life of man on earth to the time the hand of God has been at work carving the original plain. And what are the fruits of His labour? One of them is gold: gold that you and I may win. During the ages when the land where most of us were born was under ice the work went on: the rains fell and flowed to the sea; and out of all those ages of preparation and waiting one result appears to us, and that is gold."

There was an interruption or two; but the bulk of the audience clamoured for silence, and got it.

"God is just. He who robs a man of the results of his labour is a murderer to this extent that he takes a portion of his realized life. I need not remind you, my friends, of our labours in reaching this land, and the sacrifices we have made. Some of us have mortgaged our homes, even sold our all, to make this effort. Many of us have spent the best years of our adult life in this quest of nature's treasure, and in the hour of consummation have been robbed—robbed of our efforts. The result of those years has been torn from us, callously, brutally. Such corruption can only be remedied in one way. 'Thou shalt not kill,' is the Divine decree."

"But we have to get justice."

There came from the audience words of earnest agreement. The harangue of Joseph Andrews had awakened the frenzy of the crowd.

The tones and the serious presence of John Berwick appealed to their minds, while his argument wakened the thought of moral right, and, far better than rhetoric could do, steeled their resolves.

John told simply, briefly, the history of gold-mining in Australia, and of the many times corruption had wrecked individual fortunes. Justice, primarily, had to do with the rights of the individual. Countless lives had been lost in the past ages to establish that principle. The conditions in the Klondike were now worse than any that had troubled Australia; but there — as in the Klondike — the distance between the mining-fields and the seat of Government had been too great, and modes of communication too slow, to bring effective remedies. The agents of betterment found the diggings depleted, and the wrongs complained of now irreparable. But there need not be any shedding of blood, that fact he emphasized. What they must do was organize, and so win thousands to their cause against the hundreds under the orders of the established — and ineffective — authorities.

"But we need a head, a strong heart, to rule," John was saying.

"You're the man!" a voice shouted. "You're the man!" a hundred echoed.

"Parson Jack, Parson Jack! I knew he had something in him." Through the uncertain light John could distinguish Long Shorty.

So it happened that Berwick became the head of the revolutionists. As he sprang down from the bar the excited men crushed round him. He whispered a rendezvous to a dozen of the most eager, "Dawson's Dome, to-morrow, noon."

That night Smoothbore paced his room. The scandal of the Dominion Creek hillsides was known to him, and he speculated on its being the last straw on the back of that patient camel, the honest prospector. There was a knock on the door. He told the new-comer to enter. It was Sergeant Galbraith in civilian clothes.

"There was a meeting in the Borealis, to-night, sir. Joseph Andrews was talking."

"Did he say much?"

"A little more than usual, sir."

"Did he stir them up?"

"They did a lot of yelling."

"They always do when he talks. Anything else?"

"There was another speaker, sir."

"Who?"

"Don't know, sir."

"But you have charge of the Secret Service. You placed a man on his trail?"

"Yes, sir; Constable Hope."

"What did the stranger say?"

"He talked philosophy."

"Philosophy!"

"Yes; he's an Australian."

"Did he rouse them?"

"They did not say much; he held them quiet."

"Any sedition?"

"Yes, sir. He says the man who steals another man's work is a murderer, in that he takes a portion of his life; and he quoted the Bible."

The Sergeant saluted and retired. Smoothbore paced his room. A man who could silence a Dawson crowd—one who quoted the Bible—was a man to be watched! Smoothbore knew his duty; it was to his sovereign, and his sovereign's authority; it was in his province to maintain the integrity of his sovereign's empire. He knew that many of his men sympathized with the miners, and that the miners were conscious of this sympathy. He knew, also, that many of the miners believed, in the case of an uprising of the people, that the opposition of the police would be merely nominal. The question, what action he should take, had been facetiously asked him many times; but he had allowed no man to read his mind. The iniquities of the liquor-permit system were known to him, for in his official capacity he had to enforce the law. The rascality in the Gold Commissioner's office, and the graft of the toll-bridge and the Bonanza Creek trail, all—all were known to him, and were bad, bad—thoroughly bad. Villainy, barefaced or subtle, permeated officialdom, but officialdom he must protect.

There was no real hesitancy, although he recognized both sides of the question. He was going to do his duty, and he knew that his men would follow him.

Twenty men were present on the Dome at the time appointed. No one had marked their coming, and it would not have mattered if they had. Men often climbed the Dome to spy out the land or to locate the timber that grew upon its sides, for it would soon be winter, and logs were already being cut and hauled. From the Dome all who were approaching could be seen; there were no walls with ears at that place.

John moved a resolution that a council be formed, representative of the four nationalities—Australian, English, Canadian, and the United States. He and George would canvass the Australians and English. Hugh said he and Joseph Andrews would work among the Canadians. Long Shorty thought he could round up a host of Americans, and Frank Corte said he would back him up. These were men who would form the council. The first thing to do was to canvass the town and find out how many could be won to the cause, after which another meeting would be held and progress reported. Following this, the creeks were to be gone over. To prevent bloodshed the force must be overwhelming. Bonanza, Hunker, and Eldorado would probably not yield many helpers. These creeks had been staked before the advent of Poo-Bah, and the police had given records. The owners had no complaint. Nothing more than moral support could be counted from these. But on the new creeks—Dominion, Sulphur, Indian River, Australia Eureka, Too-Much-Gold, All-Gold, and the rest—there was little doubt that the support of thousands could be obtained.

On the hillsides of Bonanza and Hunker startling discoveries had recently been made. Gold Hill was proved enormously rich, Adams Hill, Magnet Hill, and Monte Cristo Hill were all of great potential wealth. The White Channel was being discovered, and the rights of location were hard to establish, if not impossible. In the gambling and dance-halls clerks of the Gold Commissioner's office were nightly to be seen squandering money on gambling and women. Their wage was two dollars per day and food, yet many of them rather lived in the hotels at a cost of fifteen dollars per diem! All this explained the difficulty of obtaining record. The rightful owners of the newly-discovered property were mostly residents of Dawson, employing lawyers in their attempt to obtain just rights. These men were the most desperate. Then there were the Forty Mile, Glacier, and Twelve Mile Creeks. There was a large number on Glacier and Forty Mile Creeks.

The nature of the discussion was necessarily wide. John insisted that they all should devote attention to the town for the first few days. Each man gained as an adherent should be questioned as to his arms and ammunition, the capacity of his rifle, and the quantity of his ammunition. Notes were to be taken of these details. Only by such means could they estimate what might be expected from the men on the creeks. The need of caution was expressed by all on all. No word of what was doing should be allowed to reach the police, and every possible adherent must be carefully sounded ere he was taken into confidence.

John tarried on the Dome after the meeting. He requested George, Frank, and Hugh to post to the home-camp and prepare a meal. A tremendous responsibility had come to him in the last few hours; and now that action had been taken he wished to meditate upon it. He had taken a great step, and could only contemplate a result far-reaching.

When the last man had disappeared among the timber below, he arose from his seat and wandered towards the wooded gulch to the north of the Dome, which he had partly explored in the days of his convalescence. He thought he remembered something. He found it again—a cleft in the rock. By the aid of a few poles and brush and a little moss it would become a fair habitation, his den!—"David therefore departed thence and escaped to the Cave Adullam ... and every one that was in distress, and every one that was in debt, and every one that was discontented, gathered themselves unto him."

Was he to be another David?

He sought the home-trail; and as he ate his meal told his companions that he would camp alone; no one else had better be with him in the Cave of Adullam.

That afternoon he placed an outfit on his back and walked to his new lonely abode. Time was precious, so he would not allow any of his companions to assist him, but rather requested that they should turn immediately to their work of organization. Besides, it was his humour to be alone.

As he chopped the trees necessary to complete his den, his mind conceived many things. Fond recollections came, and they led to a contemplation of the purposes of his life. Was he ever to be useful, creative? Instinctively his mind avoided the immediate issue of events. After all, the time for thought had given place to the time for action.

CHAPTER XXIV
WITHIN THE BARRACKS

When Constable Hope had made his report upon Berwick's abiding-place, and added to it particulars as to his visitors, and the council held on the Dome, Smoothbore recognized that he had to do with a man of more than ordinary character and intelligence. In the first place, a council held upon the Dome's summit in broad daylight was not susceptible to eavesdropping. As a base of assault upon the town, a modern rifle might drop a bullet into the barrack yard. There were possibly fifty thousand men against less than two hundred!

As a matter of fact, six hundred officers and men were on their way to the Yukon, via the Stikeen route: that is, if they had not got "cold feet" and turned back. In any case, such military outfits were of little good. Being a staunch believer in the Police, Smoothbore had little faith in the Militia!

The report of the meeting on the Dome was to the effect that council had been held and that the different parties attending it had immediately left town. Berwick's former residence had been abandoned, and its other occupants (who had been at the meeting) were not to be seen in any of the dance-halls or gambling-saloons.

Crossing the quadrangle of the Barracks from the orderly-room towards his own private office, immediately after reading the report of Constable Hope, Smoothbore met Inspector Herbert, the officer of the day.

Smoothbore returned the other's salute and stopped, which brought Herbert to a standstill also, and then, glancing over his shoulder at the Dome towering behind the town, inquired,

"Herbert, how would you like leading a squad of men against a trenched position on the top of the Dome?"

"The only way a man could storm that position would be by flying machine—and they're not invented yet. But you might cut off the enemy's supplies—that is, if you had enough men—or their water—there is no water except in the draw at the back. Were you thinking of having some manoeuvres, sir?"

"Manœuvres may be made necessary by the dread realities of war."

Herbert opened his eyes wide, and looked at his chief. Smoothbore did not return his gaze; he was still looking intently at the top of the hill, where he could see a flag-staff and the figure of a man. Herbert followed his gaze, noted the human figure, and made to take his military glasses from their case. But his superior checked him. "Don't look up there with your glasses; some one may have his on us."

"You don't mean that you seriously fear an insurrection," Herbert then exclaimed; "that these dirty prospectors will show fight?" Herbert had a contempt for the populace similar to that of Louis XV.

Smoothbore turned to him. "There are as many known murderers in Dawson as there are mounted police in the whole of the Yukon. On that hill there is a man who quotes Scripture; can probably string out his pedigree to the Conquest; and propounds the doctrine that the man who steals another's substance steals that portion of his life which went to the acquiring of that substance. This is a dangerous doctrine—because it makes our grafters murderers! The great majority of his followers will absorb this doctrine without question. Every one of the discontented is ready to lay the responsibility of his non-success on the shoulders of the officials. God knows we have real grafting and grafters enough; but if you would hear each separate tale of woe, or the different tales of woe that each malcontent will unburden himself of at the least excuse, and add the whole together, the sum would involve twice the number of claims at present made in the Yukon Valley. It does not matter that these injuries are many of them fancied: the effect upon the possessor of the delusion is the same. These men have endured countless hardships on the trail: they have—many of them—staked their all in the venture. The hopes they encouraged within themselves as they struggled to the goal have given place to dejection. Now they find themselves at the end of their resources, and their ways are blocked by corruption! Can you not understand how little organized agitation will ferment rebellion?"

"And they have abundant ammunition," commented Herbert, ever-practical.

"They brought a great supply with them, thinking to kill game on the way. They met little or none, and consequently have their ammunition unspent. Look in at any of the second-hand shops, and you will find numbers of the highest class of modern rifles, with stacks of ammunition, on sale at half their original cost."

"Then you really fear rebellion?"

"Not fear, but I think rebellion is not improbable. Officers of the mounted police don't fear anything this side of the Great Divide," and the speaker smiled.

"Would it not be well to arrest the ringleaders, and nip the thing in the bud?" asked the Inspector.

"We have no charge to lay against them, except the voicing of sedition; and there was only one man who did so. And if we did arrest him—no! it would not do! Besides: sedition!—there are enough people voicing sedition within earshot of Whitehall to keep the prisons of England filled were they all arrested. It would be a hard thing to get a jury to convict on a charge of sedition."

With this the Commandant continued his way to his office.

Smoothbore sat at his desk, and filled his pipe. His conversation with his Inspector had not dispelled his apprehensions—far from it. He must do something. He turned to the constable who was busy with papers at a neighbouring desk, and sent him for Sergeant Galbraith. In the meantime he sat and thought. There were few Canadians in the total population of the Yukon, while the English and Australians were the most bitter against the existing wrongs, and foremost in their utterances of protest.

In due time Sergeant Galbraith entered and saluted. Smoothbore turned to him,

"Constable Hope has not been able to find any trace of the associates of Berwick at their tent, nor in the dance-halls?"

"He has not, sir."

"They appear to have left town. It is clear that they are organizing, which means trouble. What is Hope doing?"

"Detailed to watch the Dome, sir."

"You had better put another man on that job, and send Hope to the Forks, and on through to Dominion, if needs be, to see if he can pick up any trace of these men, and if so to ascertain what they are doing. He might travel in plain clothes. It is possible he may give the appearance of being a likely recruit for the Klondike Free State."

"Very good, sir."

"Do you see any signs of organization?"

"Nothing further, sir."

"Well, have a look in at these second-hand shops that have the most rifles and ammunition in stock, and size up what they have. Then you can see later if much is being sold. You might ask the proprietors to find out where the purchasers say they are going. The explanation for your questions will be that you understand there has been a new find made somewhere, and that you wish to ascertain where it is."

"Very good, sir."

There could be no doubt that, if a number of rebels entrenched themselves on the summit of the Dome, there would be no dislodging them, while they could drop bullets into any part of the town, including the Police Barracks!

Smoothbore had small hopes of securing any number of recruits from the civilian population. No, the civilian population would take little hand in suppressing a rising. There was no end to be served by the Police making the first move; they could only wait and watch, hoping for something to turn up. The humour of the malcontents might change; some new distraction might spring up. The British Empire had been on the verge of collapse a score of times, but always something had happened to floor the prophets. He was quite ready to believe that the man at the head of the new movement—this John Berwick—was steadfast in his affection for the British Crown; quite possibly his action in the matter grew out of his loyalty. And being right in this reflection goes to show how worldly-wise the Police Commandant really was. That in a crisis, such as was being developed, he proved strong enough to lie low, illustrates the moral and physical courage of the man.

CHAPTER XXV
RECRUITING

That Frank, Hugh, and George had not returned to their tent the night after the council of war on the Dome was due to nothing more than the fact that they had gone to town with Long Shorty, and had stayed the night in his cabin. They did not appear in the saloons and dance-halls because they had decided upon Baxter's Free Library as down-town headquarters. Hence it was that two astute policemen had made wrong deductions; and while Constable Hope was haunting the resorts on the creeks for them, they were actually in the heart of the metropolis.

The selection of Baxter's Free Library was the result of the astuteness of Long Shorty. He knew the place. Only in Dawson would it have been worthy of the name of library, as the number of volumes was limited to a score or so. There were also several newspapers there, which, though thumbed and scrawled upon and tattered, were the latest the camp contained.

Access to these newspapers and books was free, the revenue of the establishment being derived from a lunch counter. As the building was located one street back from that which ran along the water front, the rent paid was comparatively small; and the proprietor was able to serve a roll and a cup of coffee for fifty cents, and a plate of stew, made of bully beef, or pork and beans, for a dollar and a half, which was about 33 per cent. cheaper than fashionable prices!

The combination of comparatively cheap food and free reading drew to Baxter's many of those who had ample time upon their hands, with little or no money in their pockets, and who were unwilling, or unable, to perform the heavy labour of mining operations on the creeks. They were of the educated and semi-educated classes; and among their motley members Long Shorty guessed that many desperate characters might be found. A winter—the most severe in which white people lived—would be upon them in a few short months.

The plan of campaign decided upon was that each of the four conspirators should enter the reading-room, engage in reading, and gradually draw possible recruits into conversation—which in free-and-easy Dawson would not be difficult to do.

Long Shorty was not long in picking out his man. He seemed the ordinary type of prospector, well-set-up and muscular; his dress was of good quality, by which it was to be inferred that his outfit would be large, and in all probability would include a rifle or two with ammunition. He was reading a copy of Shakespeare.

Long Shorty sat beside him, and picked up a copy of the Bible. Bibles and the works of William Shakespeare were the most common volumes in Dawson in the summer of '98. Long Shorty turned over the pages, read a verse, then put down the book, and sighed.

"Well, stranger," he said, "what do you think of things?"

"Damned bad."

"They sure are; but what are you going to do about it?"

"Just about the same as the rest; get out of the country as soon as I can. Isn't that what you're going to do?"

"I guess so—after I've made my pile!"

"Well, if you get away with a pile, I reckon you'll have to make two: one for yourself and one for the grafters."

"There may be a change."

"You must have been listening to the fellow down at the Borealis the other night."

"Perhaps I was," said Long Shorty significantly.

"And you think those fellows will ever do more than talk?"

"Well, you know how many police there are, and how many there are of the others. The police are armed with old Winchesters, twenty years behind the times! Looks like the insurrectoes might have a chance if they got together and had ammunition and rifles."

"There are lots of both among the crowd, I guess. I have a 303 and a thousand cartridges; that is, five shots for every policeman in the country." He spoke with some bitterness.

Long Shorty rightly concluded that here was a spirit who only wanted a leader. To make doubly sure he thought he would draw him a little and see how much real mutiny was in his heart; so he said,

"But there are the claim-owners, grafters, and other civilians who might aid the police."

"Not much! The claim-owners wouldn't, except possibly those who got their holdings through Poo-Bah. The fellows who got their claims straight would know a new Government would do them more good than harm."

The speaker then, as if tired of politics, pointedly went on with his reading; his mind was absorbing the philosophy of the melancholy Jacques.

Long Shorty's sensibilities were not of the finest, and he refused to consider the conversation closed; so he asked the direct question,

"What would you do if the boys got up?"

"Nothing!—I'd do nothing. It's no use considering it: I'm off down the river on a steamer leaving to-morrow. I'm going to work my way as a wood-passer to St. Michael's, after which I'll trust to luck for getting to 'Frisco. But if the boys are really going to rise, they have my good wishes. I tried to sell my rifle to-day, and the best offer I could get was five dollars—and I told the fellow I'd chuck it into the Yukon first. If you are going to stay I'll make you a present of it, to be given to the boys if they want it."

The man was going home. Long Shorty felt there was no use in attempting to hold him; so he answered in such a manner as to accept the offer, and yet not compromise himself. He said, "I don't mind taking the rifle and the cartridges and holding them in case things do happen—though I may be away on the creeks at the time."

"All right, I leave them with Baxter here; you can call for them to-morrow." Again he returned to the Forest of Arden, and Long Shorty permitted the conversation to close.

In the meantime, the other three had been hard at work. George met one Australian whose sentiments were so pronounced that he quickly closed with him; and as the recruit knew several others in the library, the agitation made good progress.

It was agreed by the reformers and the new recruits that they should all meet later in the day at Lookout Point, which was the angle of the Klondike Bluffs, where the valley of the Klondike met that of the Yukon. In later years a seat and a flag-staff were erected there, and it became a favourite trysting-place for young men and maidens engaged in another quest than that of gold.

This arrangement settled, George set off to report to Berwick, while the others, still looking for more of the rightly disaffected, drifted into the different saloons.

Berwick was delighted at their present success, and was eager to meet the party at Lookout Point. He felt that if so many adherents could be gained by such a small canvass, three or four thousand devoted armed men, at least, could be recruited from Dawson and its environs. The outlook was hopeful.

CHAPTER XXVI
LOCATED

In due course, that is three or four days afterwards, Constable Hope returned from the creeks with the report that there was no trace to be found of the allies of John Berwick. To Smoothbore this was not evidence of any abandonment of the conspiracy. He was convinced that Berwick meant business. There was, besides, a strange quietude reigning over Dawson. So mercurial a population could not have let its excitement subside and disappear in that short time.

On the other hand, Inspector Herbert was confident enough to be facetious at the expense of the enemies of officialdom. When Smoothbore told him that Hope's expedition had no result, he said,

"I thought as much; you'll find the reputed leader has some fool theory of the origin of gold, and is camped on the Dome to receive inspiration, while his followers have slipped off down the river for the good of their healths."

"Perhaps," replied Smoothbore as he glanced at the Dome. "Perhaps!" and they parted.

"The old man is a bit locoed on this rebellion theory," mused Herbert as he went along. "It's strange in a man who has seen so much service, and with him it is not 'nerves.'" Just then Herbert happened to glance up at the Dome. "By Jove! what a position for a couple of maxims. One hundred men could stand off ten thousand. I wonder! There are thousands of men starving, with many too proud to beg, and little to spare even for them. What would a successful revolution mean? For one thing, it would establish a multitude of openings in the new Civil Service—with chances of graft. It would mean a new police force, or militia, perhaps both, the members of which would, at least, be fed. It is not a case so much of righting wrong, as of getting for these fellows a piece of the pumpkin. Taking that view of it, it looks serious. What if the old man were right!" Such were the thoughts that flashed through Herbert's mind.

Almost within a minute after Smoothbore had left him he was wavering in his opinions; now he was striding in pursuit of him.

"Well—what do you think we had better do about it," asked the Commandant, after he had heard the changed opinions of his Inspector.

"Arrest the leaders!"

The conversation was interrupted by a knock at the office-door, which was followed by the entrance of Constable Hope, quite in a fluster.

"I have located Berwick's friends, sir," he reported, "in fact he was with them when I spotted them. They were all in Baxter's Free Library, and they are up to something. Berwick sits reading the Bible, and every now and then one of his aides-de-camp comes up and whispers in his ear, and then goes away to begin opening conversation with some pilgrim. I sat down, thinking one of them might come to me with his talk, but no results, sir."

"Well, now you have them located, take two good men in plain clothes and point the gang out to them; in fact, you might take four, so that henceforth they can be easily traced. Detail one man to Berwick and two to the others."

"Good man, that," remarked Herbert, when Hope had left their presence.

"Yes, it would be a pity to have him in the Army."

"My guess seems to have been wrong as to the movements of the gang."

Smoothbore made no comment on this, but asked,

"Would you arrest them now?"

"Yes."

"I am afraid I must still disagree with you," was the Chief's answer, and Herbert shortly after went away.

Constable Hope collected together four of his comrades, told them to dress in civilian clothes and follow him. They did so and joined the crowd in Baxter's. In due time the four policemen had registered in their memory the features of John Berwick and his followers. Constable Hope then told off three men according to instructions, and with the remaining policeman left the place.

"Who are those fellows?" asked the Constable who accompanied Hope.

"Berwick is the prospective liberator of the oppressed and down-trodden miner. He can talk on occasions; in fact I heard him and nearly determined to jump my uniform."

"What do they propose to do?"

"Send the police down the river, and set up for themselves!"

"Cheerful for us! Do you think they will make the effort?"

"Smoothbore seems to take them seriously, and I think Herbert is coming to think the same way."

"What will Smoothbore do?"

"Stand pat! What else would he do? What would you or I do?" and Constable Hope looked at his companion in a manner not complimentary.

"The outfit would surely get licked in the end."

"To be sure they would!—but in the meantime, two years: how much could you graft in two years?"

This query admitted of no reply, and lacking a further word from his companion, Constable Hope continued,

"Fifty miles, ten hours on the river—and you are in the land of Uncle Sam! See?"

"Yes, I see."

"If you think over it a bit you will see more."

"Yes, I guess my vision would enlarge; and you say Smoothbore is only standing pat?"

"I do."

"Funny!"

"It's not funny: it's the only thing to do; they have not begun to mass their forces yet. When they do we might have some evidence."

Shortly after Hope and Inspector Herbert had left Smoothbore, Sergeant Galbraith knocked at the office door, and reported.

"I've looked into the second-hand shops, and sized up their ammunition. Rosenbaum on Second Street reports considerable buying lately, and so does Hobson on Third Avenue. In fact, sir, they appeared to be somewhat excited. The Jew thought there was a strike up the Klondike and the Cockney thought there must be a stampede up the Stewart."

"Perhaps these stories may be right!"

"No, sir, I think not. The town patrol reported to-day two fellows in from Wind City, sir, on the Edmonton Trail, and I looked them up. They had not met any fellows going up the Stewart; that is, any number worth mentioning."

"Then this looks like corroborative evidence: at least the trouble is reaching such a stage as to make it advisable to get on the defensive; also, we must let the men know what seems likely to happen. Have the town patrol keep their eyes on all men carrying rifles."

"Very good, sir."

"Report direct to me anything that appears of interest."

"Yes, sir."

"And, Sergeant—what about those fellows who arrived from Edmonton?"

"They were in a very bad state, sir. Of their party of fourteen they were the only survivors. They wintered at Wind City, got scurvy, and all died but four, and of the four these two only remain. The other two were drowned in a rapid."

"Poor fellows! That will do, Sergeant."

Smoothbore was left to his recollections and general musings.

"Gold, gold—the price that is paid for it! Fifty thousand men in this stampede; two hundred and fifty thousand people affected; homes devastated; affections torn asunder! Hundreds dead by scurvy or drowning; thousands with constitutions wrecked! The gold is not worth the candle, with the Trusts betrayed and morals twisted! It is not worth it. Look at this little Yukon district, remote from the world. Our genesis was of gold; it would seem our dissolution will be through the same agent! The love of gold, that it may command luxury, is a source of overwhelming evil: it feeds our vices—that is pretty well all that can be said of this insensate greediness. But this is not practical!" he continued, moving. "I must give orders that the men pay special attention to their rifles and side-arms;" and he went off at once to the orderly office. The time had come for every preparation to be made. The Commandant considered the position.

There was no scope for fortifying the Barracks. The buildings were of logs, loopholes could be made by the simple process of pushing a rifle barrel through the mortar. The main thing was that the police should appear to be unconscious of the movement on foot.

One action he determined upon, and that was the purchase of the best rifles and ammunition in the shops: this to be accomplished by secret agents. This was not entirely intended to keep arms from Berwick's men, for the enemy would still have enough ammunition to exterminate the police force. But the arms of the police were not "modern"!

CHAPTER XXVII
THE WOOD-PILE

The Wood-pile was an institution almost as famous with the underworld as Dawson itself. From St. Michael's to Frisco, and up and down the Yukon River, its reputation held. At the mention of its name the pale and sickly faces of the vicious became still paler and more sickly, when they did not flush with angry hatred.

The Wood-pile was the prison, called so because the inmates, given hard labour, worked out their debt to society by sawing wood. In cold winter-weather—the winter of the sub-Arctic, with the thermometer forty degrees below zero!—the process was no joke.

The great majority of the prisoners were United States citizens, in the souls of whom many fourths of July had engendered a contempt for the British uniform. To be herded by a yellow-leg with a rifle, and made to saw wood to keep the oppressor warm, was a circumstance that rankled.

Five Ace Dan—called, for brevity's sake, Five Ace—was on the Wood-pile.

One day Five Ace was taking a hand in a Poker game, and by some mischance one of the other players detected him extracting a card from his sleeve, and charged him with the offence. There was, of course, a row, whereupon Five Ace drew a revolver, and pointed it at his adversary, with the words—adorned with some special expletives,

"If I had you across the line I'd fill you full of holes."

Whereat the man addressed came back with the words, uttered with a leer and a hiss,

"But we ain't: See!"

Five Ace was surely in hard luck, for a policeman heard the noise of the row, and quickly gathered him in. Smoothbore gave him three months on the Wood-pile, with a blue ticket at the end of that term. A blue ticket meant that the authorities requested the recipient to leave the country— an invitation rarely not taken advantage of! But Five Ace was serving his term in the summer months, when fuel was not a pressing necessity, and the number of prisoners was large. The stock employment of the gang was drawing gravel from the banks of the Yukon and carrying it in barrows to the quadrangle of the Barracks, or the road-bed of the main street.

While climatic conditions were infinitely better during the summer months than they were in winter, this was not an unmixed blessing to Five Ace; for while the winter months were dark and drear and cold, the coldness, darkness, and dreariness, together with the abundance of clothing it was necessary for the prisoners to wear, made it hard for their persons to be recognized by passers-by. On the other hand, during the bright summer days, the situation was very embarrassing; and it is easy to believe that any one holding strong ideas on the rights of man, a true citizen, that is to say, of the United States, so imprisoned, was ready for any desperate venture. If it came to the killing of a yellow-leg or two—what matter? There were no greater or more glorious people on God's green earth than the citizens of the United States! Five Ace was quite ready to pose as a hero and martyr, when opportunity served.

Long Shorty happened to be a friend of Five Ace Dan; not that he consorted with tin-horns, but Dan hadn't always been what he was now, and, anyway, there wasn't much harm in pulling off a trick once in a while! The officials in this country were always robbing people, so why should not he put in a hand?

One day, as Long Shorty was prospecting for recruits, he recognized Five Ace among the gang employed in the gravel pit, and, quick as a flash, the idea came that it would be well to have an ally among the prisoners. How to get into communication with Five Ace was a matter demanding consideration; it would not do to make a mess of things through any little mistake at the beginning. So he walked away, pondering, and sat down and reviewed the situation from afar; in other words, he watched the prisoners and noted their movements. There were about eight in this particular band, over whom stood a policeman. The process was for the prisoners to file down to the shore of the river, fill their barrows, and march back again. Each man returned to the spot he had left and picked up the tools he had been working with.

The best means to get a word with Five Ace was by means of a note, provided the note did not fall into the hands of the police! Long Shorty soon came to his decision. The note must not be compromising. This is what Long Shorty wrote,

"The Marmot has generally two entrances to his burrow, the yellow-leg has only one. Some day soon something is going to happen, but in the meantime the hunters with rifles would like to know if the yellow-legs are wise to the game. Where the seed is sown there will the flower grow, and I expect response to this where I sow it; at dinner-hour I will look for it."

After setting down this on a piece of paper, Long Shorty, not a little proud of his achievement, rumpled it up with another piece of blank paper and enclosed a small piece of lead pencil. This was because prisoners were not always allowed paper and pencil.

After the little parcel was ready Long Shorty walked down-stream to where there was a canoe belonging to a man he knew. He borrowed the craft and began poling up-stream towards the mouth of the Klondike.

He had noted that the site of Five Ace's labour was very near the river, so that when he passed the spot he could have stepped on the tools with which the convict worked.

A labourer toiling with pick and shovel first loosens the soil with the pick and then uses the shovel. The astute mind of Long Shorty conceived that if he dropped the paper close to where the hand of the toiler, as he grasped the shovel, would be, events would work out—as they did.

Five Ace, on returning with the empty barrow, took up his pick and began to work, and while he was scratching the ground in the leisurely manner of the convict his eye saw the paper. He judged that its appearance was possibly connected with Long Shorty, who was hanging about watching. So, with the slyness proper to his fraternity, he took up the shovel and managed to smuggle and hide away the parcel by slipping it down his neck.

When Five Ace had an opportunity he read the missive, and his breast swelled. Here was evidently an invitation for him to join a rising against the oppressors! If successful it would mean that an honest fellow could shoot down a black-leg and get away. Judge Lynch would sit in the Yukon. By all means things must be kept quiet. Five Ace felt sure he could get the other prisoners to turn against their guard when the proper time came. One man might get shot; but if he were careful it need not be himself.

Long Shorty had the idea that Five Ace Dan and his fellow prisoners might, in the case of a rising outside, carry out some portion of a general move by striking a blow within. On the other hand, while Five Ace believed he was the child of a race of patriots and felt himself a champion of liberty with a possibility of shining before posterity, his first and foremost idea was always his own liberty!

He wrote a note and left it as directed, where Long Shorty secured it, and this is what it said,

"The Beaver is working with no thought of danger. If his dam is broken in spots he will fix it. To drive him out you must make a clean job. You have friends who will help, but you must keep them posted."

Five Ace had evidently the same ideas as the leader of the insurrection, that a sudden display of force, thousands strong, would make the position at the Barracks untenable and force a surrender.

The following day Long Shorty replied,

"Many years ago the south face slid off the Dome and many ingins went to the happy hunting-grounds. Some day something may slide off the Dome and keep on going till it hits the Barracks and bumps it into the Klondike. I will look out for things that are to happen, so that those in the Barracks will know what to prepare for. In case they can help, I will let them know."

All of which duly fell into the hands of Five Ace Dan, and conveyed to him the true situation of affairs. Had it fallen into those of the police it would have appeared as mere nonsense—the scribbling of some prospector whose hardships had affected his reason. That is what Long Shorty thought.

CHAPTER XXVIII
A COUNCIL OF WAR

Within a few days fifteen hundred men in Dawson had signified their readiness to act for a new Government. Another thousand could readily be counted upon from the creeks. Twenty-five hundred well-armed and determined men, entrenched at the top of the Dome, could withstand an army. To attack them, armed as they were with long-range sporting rifles, would be, on the part of the police, madness.

It was noon on a Saturday when Long Shorty left his last note to Five Ace Dan on the Yukon gravel bar. Having satisfied himself that the missive had fallen into the proper hands, he set out for the Dome to report. He found Berwick, Hugh Spencer, Bruce, Corte, and several others holding a council of war. Berwick was giving instructions.

"Behind the Dome, you will notice, is a valley where the timber is comparatively heavy. Our men can camp there with two weeks' provisions. Every man—or two men—will be their own commissariat. Their instructions will be to hold themselves in readiness while recruits are being gathered from the creeks."

"Recruits! We don't want no recruits from the creeks," roared Long Shorty. "Fifteen hundred men will fix the thing."

Hugh agreed with this. "Fifteen hundred men should be able to scare less than two hundred into surrender, especially when we can show them that we can shoot and be out of range of their rifles." Berwick put the matter to the vote, and it was agreed that the fifteen hundred to be recruited from Dawson would be sufficient.

Berwick sighed. "Very good; fifteen hundred let it be; but we must try to avoid bloodshed. This affair will be serious enough without anybody being killed. Pass the word for a muster right away; camps to be made in the woods as if a base for prospecting. At the camps rifles may be cached to be quickly available. It is possible the police may not notice the migration; but we must chance that. Until it is time to act the men will go into town every day as usual."

"Don't you think we had better have a preliminary muster?" asked George.

"Yes. It would serve a double purpose: give an opportunity to our men to learn the plans; and the massing of so many upon the Dome would doubtless lead to inquiries by the police, and probably impress them with our display of force. It is hardly possible they will make arrests, and they can hardly shoot unarmed men."

"It won't do 'em any harm to show we look like meaning business. Why not have the boys bring their arms?" asked Long Shorty.

"I'd say nothing about arms," Hugh counselled. "Let each man suit himself; there'll be enough guns in the crowd to guard against accidents."

"And what are we to do after our display of force?" asked Long Shorty.

"Send a letter to the Barracks, calling on the officer commanding to surrender," answered John Berwick.

"If he does not surrender? Suppose he tells you to go to the devil?"

"We'll give him till Saturday to consider it."

"And then, if he says no?"

"He won't say no: he is a humane man, and must know we are in the right. He must also be aware that we can annihilate him."

Berwick did not quite possess the assurance he showed in this reply. There might be such a thing as Smoothbore being willing to die at his post. Of late this idea had been more and more gaining hold on his mind; his sleep had become more restless as the time for action approached. In all probability some irresponsible person would make a slip, which would precipitate matters.

Dark thoughts and doubts came upon him, as they must at times to every leader who holds under his control many lives; but resolutely he put them from him, and comforted his heart, strengthened his determination, by remembering the wrongs they had suffered and the righteousness of their cause. He hoped earnestly that Smoothbore would recognize that his force was outnumbered by at least ten to one.

But Long Shorty was tenacious; possibly he thought he detected some wavering in his leader. And so he persisted,

"But if he does call the bluff?"

"In that case we must hold a council of war, and determine what to do. Our display of force on Wednesday should make him apprehensive. By Friday our intentions and strength must have impressed him. Then we shall forward him a summons to surrender! If by Saturday noon he has not complied...."

"We'll drop a few bullets round the flag-pole," cried Long Shorty; "and it would not do much harm if we peppered a yellow-leg or two."

"I'd rather they got one of the grafters!" said a recruit, to which remark others chorused, "Hear! hear!"

"We'll see—we'll see! What we need first is to get our forces camped in the woods. So pass the word among our adherents that they are expected to gain their encampment during Monday and Tuesday. Let Sunday be a day of rest; it is possible the Sunday after may be far from peaceful!"

"All right, boss," spoke up Frank. Frank was far more loyal to "Parson Jack," much less inclined to question him, than Long Shorty.

"That ends this present business," said John. "Those of you who don't wish to go into town may as well stay and go over the ground in survey of a line of entrenchment."

Thereupon, with his friends about him, John went to his den and secured a pick and shovel hidden there, and with them traced a furrow, to be enlarged later. The riflemen would lie there and fire upon the Barracks. To this day that furrow is to be found across the top of the Dome.

Dawson was now at the zenith of its prosperity. Not only had the creeks produced many millions, but vast sums of outside capital were being paid for speculative claims, as well as for properties of proven worth. For those who were prosperous it was a heyday of delight; to those whose fortunes had stuck it was no heyday. It was for these that Berwick and his comrades were working: to give honest workers something of a fair chance; though there was a long span between the idealism of John and the motives of Long Shorty, which were not a little selfish and sordid.

There have been many popular outbursts in the world's history; but never had a leader entered his fortunes against an established Government with the chances of success held by Berwick! In numbers, in arms and equipment, he had the advantage. His hesitation was, therefore, not due to any shirking of the issue. He was the reverse of a moral coward; and yet he felt keenly the responsibility and unpleasantness of the part he had to play in leading a force against the authority of Britain's Queen. It was duty which drove him against his patriotic instincts. He loathed the necessity; but there was no alternative if wrongs were to be righted.

The five colleagues had been thoughtfully watching Dawson, that hive of human bees.

The first to break the silence was Long Shorty, when he told of his acquaintanceship with Five Ace Dan on the Wood-pile, and added the suggestion that he might prove useful. This roused Hugh, who said sharply, "We don't want any jail-birds!"

"He's a bit of a tin-horn," protested Shorty, "but he ain't a jail-bird."

"There ain't much difference," was Hugh's retort. Long Shorty held his peace.

CHAPTER XXIX
STONY GROUND

Constable Hope had no doubts. Professional instinct told him there was an important conspiracy hatching. He was ambitious, and he loved his work, so that every impulse prompted him to find and follow the threads of the plot. Smoothbore's action in keeping "tab"[10] on the number of men carrying rifles suggested to him that his Commandant regarded the situation as serious.

[10] Watch.

Therefore, beyond his orders—which were sufficient in themselves to work off an ordinary policeman's superfluous energy—Hope worked overtime. He discovered that George, Hugh, and Frank occupied the home-ranch once more, and were extremely busy. He reasoned that if a man's business be legitimate, it is easy to learn its nature. As the business of these men was not quite evident, he determined to find out what it was. So that on the morning of the meeting at the Dome Hope had made his way there also, by a detour to the east. His route was the longer, and the sun was hot. Also the trail he took led through some patches of swamp, which meant mosquitoes.

When he reached the nearest point to the Dome, where he could remain under cover of the bush, he was still out of earshot. He watched those who came in view, but because the council had been seated in a circle about the summit, after the manner of the Indian pow-wow, and he was below the level of that summit, he could see only some of those who had attended.

After the meeting had dissolved, and those remaining had plotted out their entrenchments and started to return to Dawson, Hope made bold to follow them. He drew back in time to avoid discovery from the five who still were gazing thoughtfully upon the town; but he happened to hear the reference to Five Ace Dan and the Wood-pile.

"They're camped on our trail. Five Ace would hardly be in demand for a prayer meeting," thought the guardian of the peace, as eventually he returned to the Police Barracks. He at once reported to Sergeant Galbraith.

"The big Tyee[11] held a council of war on the summit at noon to-day. These fellows are sure up to something."

[11] Chinook for Chief.

"Hear anything?"

"No; could not get near enough, except at the last, when the big Yankee said something about Five Ace Dan."

"Who's he?" asked Galbraith.

"The tin-horn on the Wood-pile for pulling a gun. Well, the Yankee said something about his helping their cause or something; and the one they call Hugh said he had no use for tin-horns. It looks as if the Yankee might be in communication inside the Barracks."

"Well, he wouldn't learn much."

"He might tell them how poor are our arms."

"They know that already," Galbraith snorted.

"And how weak our guard is."

"They know that, too. That's the reason of this insurrection, or one of the reasons. But what has a reference to Five Ace Dan got to do with this plot that is supposed to be going on?"

"Nothing, I guess. Probably nothing!"

"Well, the only thing you have to report is, that there was a pow-wow on the Dome this morning."

"I guess so."

"But whether they were planning to put us all out of business, or organizing an expedition to the North Pole—you don't know."

"That's right."

"Well, keep your eye on them, but don't report again until your report is calculated to make a noise."

Constable Hope, not a little discouraged by the way his report was received, sauntered out and drifted towards the Borealis. The seeds of his efforts had fallen on stony ground.

But after he was gone Sergeant Galbraith expanded his chest, drew up to the full extent of his six feet, and gazed through the door of his office at the muskeg, which did duty for a street.

"Another council at the top of the Dome," he said to himself. He stood a minute, stroked his moustache; then, his mind made up, strode out of the office, and in due course was in the presence of his Commanding Officer.

"Another council at the Dome, sir," he reported.

"Yes."

"Seems serious, sir, when men climb 1,800 feet, this hot weather, that they may talk in private."

"Any other signs, Sergeant?"

"It's the other signs that make it look serious. The number of men carrying rifles is increasing rapidly. Yesterday no less than three hundred rifles were seen in the streets."

"Did you question any of those carrying them?"

"No, sir. Had no orders, sir."

"Just so: it would not have done any good, and it might have done harm. And you have had all supplies bought up, arms and ammunition?"

"All that were better than our own, sir."

"Well, have them secretly brought to the men's quarters, and let each man have his pick. Then some of the best shots can have a day off to practise a bit."

"Very good, sir."

"Something is going to happen soon," said Smoothbore to Herbert, who during the interview had come in.

"Rather suggestive of Micawber that, if you will pardon my saying so," Herbert ventured to assert. He had been a sudden and complete convert to the theory that trouble was brewing. The inaction of his Chief had been getting on his nerves.

"Micawber had the great virtue of patience," answered Smoothbore with a smile.

"I would arrest the leaders, sir, on a trumped-up charge, and get the evidence out of them that way."

"That would be a mistake, my dear Herbert."

"Perhaps so, sir; but here they can shoot us down like rats. If we have to die, we had better die like men."

"If something does not turn up—as, you remind me, Micawber might have said—you will have sufficient opportunity to die."

"I should wish to sell my life pretty dearly sir!"

"Perhaps you won't have to sell it at all—if the something happens that I expect."

"What do you expect, sir, may I ask?"

"Just something," and Smoothbore smiled again. After a pause he continued, "By all the laws of military and political science the British Empire should have been wrecked ages ago. But something always has happened. To arrest the leaders of this conspiracy would, I am sure, be an error. It would precipitate matters, and undoubtedly cause bloodshed. You must remember it is not with redskins we are dealing. Many of these fellows who are arraying themselves against us are excellent shots, accustomed to rough life, and in every way calculated to make good fighters in such a country as this. If they really take up arms against us, there is nothing to do but fight—fight to the death, sell our lives as dearly as possible, as you say. If they have no intention of taking up arms—and it is not yet certain that they will—we can suffer no harm by inaction."

"We might buy the leaders."

"A man who would sell himself and his friends would not stay bought; and, somehow, I do not feel that the integrity of the British Empire should be maintained by purchasing her enemies."

"But then there are our lives!"

"Our lives don't figure in this proposition," and once again Smoothbore smiled.

Herbert felt his Chief was trifling with him and with the situation, so he rose from his chair, walked to the window, and looked out upon the quadrangle. This movement hid the flush of annoyance that had come over his face. He made an excuse, and found his way out of the office.

"If only I were in command here," he thought, "I'd clap these fellows on the Wood-pile, and then——"

After that point no well-defined line of action suggested itself to him.

Meanwhile, Smoothbore continued writing his report to Ottawa, telling of his suspicions, and explaining his action, or want of action. He intended to hold back the communication until the last moment—until he was satisfied that "something would not turn up," which would certainly be close to the crisis. Then he would confide it to a trusty scout and send to the "outside." While he was writing his mind constantly played with the facts of his own position. It pleased him to compare it with that of Gordon in Khartoum; with these differences, that, for him, assistance was out of the question, and his enemies were not fanatical and were Christian. His would be a soldier's death, if "something did not turn up."

CHAPTER XXX
ON THE SCENT

After being snubbed by his Sergeant Constable Hope lost heart—for a little while; but on the Sunday he was again working assiduously, with little luck.

Accident and caution caused Berwick to keep out of the way of the determined policeman.

Suddenly the idea of looking further into the possible connection of Five Ace Dan with the conspirators occurred to Hope. So on the day following his Sunday of ill-success he posted himself near the prisoners. He could distinguish the person of Five Ace Dan, and watched closely for any sign made to a possible confederate, but without result. This was disappointing, for brooding during the night on what Long Shorty had said, he brought himself to believe he was close to an important clue. As his inspection of Five Ace Dan brought no help to him he felt again discouraged, and became sullen and brooding. Then his interest awoke again, for Long Shorty had appeared upon the scene. The constable was about to rise to his feet and abandon the enterprise when he saw the new-comer. He hid himself again immediately.

He watched Long Shorty take a piece of paper out of his pocket and write. The man laboured hard over the missive; he was evidently no fluent scribe. The paper, after being finished and carefully read through, was rolled into a ball.

At last, at stroke of noon, the prisoners filed back to the Barracks. Long Shorty at once strolled over, with careful casualness, to the scene of their labours, and, as before, dropped the paper beside the handle of the Five Ace's shovel. At once he went eager as a bird to Dawson.

When the coast was quite clear Hope came from his cover and annexed the letter. The policeman's spirits were very cock-a-whoop.

"The Eagle is very fond of Yellow-legs," he read in the awful scrawl, "and in two days' time a great many Eagles will gather together about the summit of the big mountain, where they may watch the Yellow-legs; and if the Yellow-legs don't come and make peace within two days, then at the end of one more day the Eagles will descend upon the Yellow-legs and make a meal of them. Any little dicky-birds found among the Yellow-legs may go the same way, unless they make a move for liberty. The Eagle loves liberty."

Constable Hope pondered over these words, and after copying them into his notebook replaced the original where he had found it. He then made his way to his Sergeant and the mid-day meal. No sooner, however, had he come to Galbraith than he changed his mind. He would carry his news to the Commandant himself, and not waste it on this discouraging minor light.

"You're somewhat glum. Seen a ghost?" asked the Sergeant.

"No, Sergeant, no!"

"Been drinking the wrong kind of hootch, I guess!"

"No, Sergeant, no!"

The first thing Hope did after lunch was to search the cell occupied by Five Ace Dan. There he found, stuffed between the logs which comprised one wall of the cell, the first missive written by Long Shorty. He searched but could discover nothing else, but that would do. Off he went to the Commandant.

"I have discovered something, sir, which I have thought sufficiently important to bring direct to you."

"What is it?"

"One of the men I am watching is communicating with a prisoner—Five Ace Dan. I heard him mention the name on the Dome, on Saturday. To-day I followed up the clue and intercepted a note."

Constable Hope took out his notebook. He was a bit nervous and excited. He knew he was running a risk by not reporting, according to regulations, by way of the Sergeant. Smoothbore was eyeing him intently.

Constable Hope handed the letter found in the cell, and his notebook containing the copy of the missive left that morning, to the Commandant, who read them with stern eyes.

"You think these are not the idle words of some partially demented prospector?"

"I do not, sir. The big Yankee has nothing about him to indicate he has lost his wits."

"So you think this is right, that there will be a massing of forces about the Dome on Wednesday?"

"I do, sir."

"And if there is a display of force on Wednesday, an attack will be made on Friday?"

"On Saturday, sir."

"On Saturday; then if we see a massing of forces on Wednesday we may expect trouble by Saturday?"

"That is my idea, sir."

"What have you done with the original of the note you found to-day?"

"Put it where I found it, sir."

"And what do you intend doing with the one you found in the prisoner's cell?"

"I had thought to replace it, sir."

"Very good; we can see if to-day's note is hidden in the same place to-morrow."

Constable Hope was a proud man as he strode along the bank of the Yukon to the town. He had ventured much, and won. Visions of himself holding a commission passed through his mind. The possibility seemed more tangible now. Whom should he meet but the Sergeant?

"Well, young fellow, been hunting for more noiseless reports?"

"I've been keeping my eyes open."

"Seen anything?"

"Nothing much to trouble you with, Sergeant."

"Well, I've seen something I couldn't help but see. A stampede seems to have set in to the top of the Dome. Scores of fellows have been climbing up there, packs on their backs. You had better join the crowd."

"Not a bad idea."

In fifteen minutes Constable Hope had reached the Town Station, and made a roll of some blankets, in which he stowed several tins of bully beef and some biscuits. He was just setting out when his Sergeant arrived.

"Are not you going to take a rifle?"

"I hadn't thought of doing so."

"You'd better: all the others have rifles."

"You didn't tell me."

"Then I tell you now. No—not the police rifle," as Hope picked up a carbine. "Take this sporting rifle. Don't let 'em see you are a policeman, and use your wits!"

Hope strapped on his bundle—it weighed full sixty pounds—and with a "Good-bye, kid," from his Sergeant was off.

He made a detour far up the Klondike to gain a more gradual ascent, and on the way did a powerful lot of thinking. The fact that many men were climbing the Dome was some foundation for the idea that a gathering was to take place there on Wednesday. He sat down to rest on the flat, or, as it was called in the diggings, bench, half-way up the Klondike bluffs. There was ample time, for it was still the season of perpetual light; and if he awaited some other pilgrim would certainly come along, from whom he might find out something. Sure enough a recruit to the forces of the rebellion came into sight before five minutes had passed. The man was heavily laden and struggling up the steep ascent. He clawed at the brush in his efforts to pull himself up; and when finally he succeeded flung himself down by the side of the policeman, his face streaming with perspiration.

"A fellow will need a fat job when things get righted to pay for this!"

"He sure will," said Hope.

"I'm looking for a job collecting gold-dust."

"But there won't be any royalty then."

"That's right; that's right," and a thoughtful look came into the man's eye. "I was promised a job—I wonder what kind of a job I can get? I really had made up my mind to hold out for a job collecting. It must be an all-fired good job if a fellow reckons on the dust these fellows who hold it now blow in on the girls and wine. One year would be enough for me: I'd save, and quit the country."

"Are you quite sure you'd save?"

"Sure thing, I'm sure—at least I think I'm sure."

"Now don't you think if you were given the job of collecting royalty, that you might feel tempted to go to a restaurant, order a steak with chechacho potatoes,[12] and buy a bottle of wine to round things off?"

> [12] Fresh potatoes as distinguished from evaporated potatoes.

The man gazed into vacancy a bit, and then looked Hope in the eye, and slapped his knee, as he said,

"Do you know, partner, I think I might—if I get any boodle out of this thing that's coming off, I think I will. Beefsteak! Beefsteak and onions!—and chechacho potatoes! Gosh! what a lay-out of them I could eat right now. Beans—beans—bacon and beans—and then beans and bacon! What a hell of a lot a fellow misses in this here country!"

"Yes, but I'm afraid we will not be able to take our appetites with us."

"Say! I wonder what John D. Rockefeller would give for my appetite and my stomach! Say! I bet he'd give a million cold cash. I bet he'd give a million and a half—enough to buy the best claim on Eldorado."

"Perhaps—perhaps; but never mind, there's a good time coming for us." Constable Hope did not wish the conversation to merge too much upon the abstract.

"Yes—in one week more—then we will have a chance to do some grafting. And I tell you I can do with some; yes, sir!"

"You mean it will be all over in two weeks? As I understand it, there is to be something doing on Wednesday."

"Only a line up, as I understand it; then on Friday the boss sends them word to quit, giving them twenty-four hours to make up their minds whether they will go to Heaven or down the River."

"Yes, I guess that's the programme," said the policeman, successfully hiding the satisfaction that made his pulses throb. He felt this was the official plan, as it coincided so well with the terms of the letter now again folded in its place in the cell of Five Ace Dan.

Had Hope been without orders, he would have made an excuse, and posted back to town right away. But his Sergeant had told him to masquerade among the rebels; and he must obey orders.

So he resumed the upward march with the remark, "Well, pard, I guess we had better hit the trail," whereupon the pard, with the accompaniment of numerous oaths and grunts and sighs, struggled to his feet and onward up the hill.

CHAPTER XXXI
AN ODIOUS DILEMMA

Smoothbore was in possession of the facts Constable Hope had been able to gather, which were, indeed, very little less than the complete plot. Fifteen hundred men were camped in the bushes at the back of the Dome, with enough bullets to kill the Standing Army of the British Empire; and he had available a few more than one hundred men! True, they were good men; but so were most of those on the other side. The trouble was that both parties were right. It was for him and his men to subdue this rebellion because it threatened the integrity and honour of the Empire. At the same time the "insurrectoes" were demanding simple justice. It was an odious dilemma.

In his mind's eye he pictured the vast spaces that stretched between the Klondike and the "outside." They could hardly seem farther away from help if the Klondike were on the planet Mars. Well, he would not surrender; it would be better to die. The Yukon was sweeping along but a stone's throw from the gate of the Barracks; in eight or ten hours its rapid course would carry them into the United States. That might be a resource of security to his men, if they were beaten, but for himself he would fill a grave in that region of eternal frost.

It was Tuesday evening, the sun was sinking in the north, Heaven's vault was finely painted in pink. The abrupt cliff on the west of the Yukon threw a deep shadow across the mighty river, whose stately flood had long held sovereignty in that weird land of dreams. The light from the clouds above struggled against the shadows in the river, and was blended with them. It was certainly majestic, magnificent!

The Commandant, as he walked up and down his office, often paused to gaze upon the familiar scene.

A knock on the door caused him to start round. It was Herbert.

"I came to inquire, sir, for any fresh news on the situation."

"The news is, Herbert, that we may as well prepare to die a soldier's death. There is to be a display of force to-morrow, and mobilization on Friday, when a request to surrender will be sent in. Hostilities will open on Saturday."

"What will be their demands?"

"That the police and all Government officials quit the country; in other words, 'go down the river.'"

"And you will not comply?"

"I will not comply."

"Can nothing be done, sir?"

"Nothing but to fight to the last drop of blood."

"And the ultimate result?"

"Anyhow, we shall have upheld the prestige of the British uniform." There was a pause. Both men were very thoughtful. The Commandant then asked, "You remember Child?"

"Yes."

"He followed orders. He rode to death, because his orders were to arrest, not to shoot: he did not flinch before the levelled rifle. What he did as an individual the hundred and fifty of us can do."

"But we shall shoot!"

"We shall! While a cartridge remains and a finger has strength to pull a trigger!"

Herbert looked glum: he was not a coward, but he thought his Chief's policy was all wrong, and he was to give up his life—or die in ignominy. It made him bitter—and then his mind travelled across the great stretch of glacier, mountain, and plain, to his little cottage on the Prairie: it was not cowardice that brought the moisture to his eyes!

"Damn it all, sir, it's hard to die here like a rat in a trap," Herbert cried. He did not share his Chief's idealism. "Promise to force the Commissioner to bring some sort of order out of chaos and clear out the Gold Commissioner's office."

Smoothbore knew of the cottage and the little girl with golden curls who was all the world to the inspector; so he understood the emotion of the other and felt sympathy.

"Reform!—a promise of reform at this stage of the game would be no good. The leader of this movement is an idealist, a fanatic, and three-quarters of his followers—luck having been against them—hope to restore their fortunes by the experiment of a new Government. The situation is not dissimilar to that in the Thirteen Colonies at the Revolution: a leader of parts, of education, imbued with theories on the rights of man, at the head of a mob thirsting for the lands and jobs of the Loyalists! Why has Alaska a population? Because the Sheriff back East could not shoot straight.[13] Why had America a population before the Revolution? Because there were not prisons enough in Europe. In fact, the situation in the Klondike to-day is much the same as it was in America before the Revolution—only perhaps there is more justice on the side of these, our enemies, than there was on the side of the Yankees. The Government of George III taxed tea—which was then much more of a luxury than it is to-day: our Government taxes the one product of our people."

[13] A common saying in the North.

It was a long speech for the Commandant, but he knew what he was talking about. Herbert sighed.

"Any special orders, sir?" he asked.

"No. The men have been given their new arms, and the situation is pretty well understood among them."

"They are in fine fettle, sir, and spirit?"

"Good! If, as I expect, hostilities open, and things look hopeless, I shall give every man the opportunity of passing out and down the river, and this will include officers—but as for surrender, I won't."

Herbert, about to make his adieu, turned towards the door, when the Chief remarked,

"It appears a prisoner, known as Five Ace Dan, has been receiving communications from one of the leaders of the rising. I have given orders that a double guard be put on these men, and special sentries, to see that no word passes among them. You will see that those orders are carried out."

"Yes, sir; good-night, sir."

"Good-night, Herbert."

Smoothbore gazed at the river once again. It swung on its majestic course, but the rose tints were gone; only the dark shadows of the hill remained. The hour seemed ominous.

CHAPTER XXXII
A DERELICT

Surgeon-Major Peel was strongly imbued with the instincts of humanity, but, like many professional men, his business acumen was small. While one or two of his patients were prosperous claim-owners who could afford to pay an ounce and a half of gold-dust per day, there were many who passed into his care who could not pay, and these, the poorly nourished and mentally depressed, were the more susceptible to attacks by the deadly typhoid-bacillus.

Not that the patients were dishonest—they simply had not the money. What could be done under the circumstances? The delirious victim who was bundled up to the doors of St. George's could not be turned away! Obviously it was the duty of the Government, reaping enormous revenues from the whisky traffic and the gold royalty, to pay.

One day—it was the Tuesday before the meeting on the Dome—a big hulk of a man joined the patients of the St. George's Private Hospital. His temperature was 104½, and he was delirious. A neighbour had brought him; his name was unknown, his residence was given as the North End. It was Long Shorty!

"Poor fellow," remarked the Surgeon-Major sympathetically, when he had taken his pulse, had slipped the thermometer under his arm, and was watching the gasping figure.

"Typhoid attacks even the strongest. What a handsome animal he would be if his face showed less dissipation!"

"He does not look likely to prove a profitable guest," Alice commented. She was the housekeeper of the establishment and found the domestic problems more difficult than her father imagined.

"Who knows, who knows! He may have property which will turn out a Bonanza; think of Gold Hill—ten English pounds to each shovelful of dirt dug from the bed-rock, and the claim-owners round about were coming to the two Swedes who owned the claim to ask them to work for wages!"

"Yes, father," said Alice, "but there's another side to these stories. Think of the thousands in and around Dawson living on one meal a day; it is always the same in every mining excitement. It is either too much wealth, or nothing at all!"

She was evidently thinking of John, remembering his talk of experiences. Her father, who, though blind to many of the aspects of life, was a keen observer of his daughter, guessed at the truth.

"It is strange we can learn nothing of John," he said.

"He must be away on the creeks," she answered wistfully. "I have sent several letters to him through the post; and it can't be that they all would go astray."

The girl sighed, and her father busied himself anew with the work of the hospital.

"Fred is to give this man a cold bath and put him in ward 'C.' I really must see the Commissioner—Hi-u Bill, they call him—and come to some understanding as to indigent patients."

For some reason, not apparent on the surface, Long Shorty made a great impression upon Alice. She interested herself in his case, and often sat by his bed. His fever remained high and persistent; he was still delirious. Wild things he said. What most interested Alice was his continuous references to "Parson Jack."

"Parson Jack, I knew he was no tenderfoot; a fellow what would mush forty-five miles for a sick pal—Parson Jack—and then want to mush back again. Parson Jack, Parson Jack—he gave Poo-Bah hell—hell on toast!— Parson Jack!" And the great muscles would stand out upon his neck and arms as he waved his clenched fists in the air.

"Parson Jack" might mean any one, thought Alice.

The fever had run about a week of its course when Long Shorty entered the hospital, so that the disease had another two weeks to run before the crisis would be reached. There was nothing to do but wait patiently for the return of consciousness. In the meantime, her imagination pictured much. She tried, by suggestion, to shape the course of his ravings, but found they were as fleeting and volatile as the changing winds of the heavens.

The special services rendered by Alice to Long Shorty did not escape her father's notice. He remarked to her one day,

"Alice, no one could accuse you of worldliness; you certainly are giving the delirious patient in ward 'C' a full measure of attention!"

"Do you know, father," she then said frankly, "in some ways he reminds me of John. I don't know how it is; I suppose they have something in common, something may link them together. He is perpetually calling on Parson Jack."

"Ha!" snorted her father. "Our patient is far from being of the type of Berwick!"

Both of them hurried away to their work.

That same evening, hours after the day-staff had ceased their labours, Alice was watching beside Long Shorty, and, notwithstanding its many disagreeable passages, listened to his wild flow of language. He was ever living over again his struggles with the forces of Nature, with his fellows, and his own tempestuous passions!

"The blue water, the blue water, keep her to the blue!"—her patient was again living a dash through a rapid in a canoe.—"White water means rocks and death—death—death, I say! To the right!"—and he would shout. In those anxious weary hours the girl grew to realize something of the wild, rough life of the frontiersmen.

On the morning of the Friday when the ultimatum was to be sent to Smoothbore, Peel returned to the hospital from the town. He was in a condition of excitement, as was every one else in Dawson.

"Alice, that typhoid fellow was talking about Parson Jack?"

"He was," replied Alice, opening her eyes with expectancy. "Why do you say that?"

"Because that's the chap who is trying to overthrow the Government. Our patient may be one of the conspirators."

"Possibly," said Alice, and hastened away. She knew "Parson Jack" was Berwick. Intuition told her so. She was absolutely certain of the fact.

The news that a plot was brewing had, of course, penetrated the walls of the hospital. Now that Alice knew John Berwick was concerned in it her interest quickened and her anxieties awoke.

CHAPTER XXXIII
TRIBUTE

The demonstration of force, as organized by Berwick, had taken place according to schedule. The display was plainly seen from the Barracks, and its intent generally known throughout the town, wherein it became the one topic of conversation. The dance-halls were but half patronized, the gambling-tables seemed to have lost their popularity on that Wednesday night.

Not that any fear was felt. The men of Dawson were generally not of the fearing type. They were thirsty for news; their interest was so stirred that they must let off steam by talking.

In the Borealis the woman nicknamed Roundeyes stood apart. Of all the faces present hers alone showed apprehension, for she had a real regard for Poo-Bah, the Prince of Grafters, whose domination at last was threatened.

Suddenly her eyes lit up. A big hulk of a man came stumbling into the place. Poo-Bah! Her face grew white as she ran up and caught his arm.

"What—what will they do with you?" she asked.

"Nothing, I guess." He laughed in a rambling manner. "What do they want me for?"

"Some fellow you have done up will take a shot at you now there is no danger of the yellow-legs!"

Until the present crisis the prestige of the police had been so great that the possibility of any one seeking and gratifying personal revenge had never crossed Poo-Bah's mind. What would happen now? With all his confidence the question asked by the girl would repeat itself. He knew he was not popular. Many a man owed the wreck of his fortune to him, and would enjoy a chance of shooting him. His hands clenched for a minute, but he put the thought away. It was the spirit of the voyageur, the custom of the country, to brush aside the disagreeable. The thought of death and of what may come after death was resolutely set aside.

"Oh, hell! Come and have a drink." So he endeavoured to disperse his own and the woman's fears. She was not so easily satisfied. She caught him again by the arm, bowed her head against his shoulder, and sobbed,

"Oh, my baby! my baby! Somebody will blow daylight through you!"

Poo-Bah drew his arm roughly from her with the single word "Quit!" and strode towards a curtained recess, Roundeyes meekly following. In a minute or two a champagne bottle popped, and there was laughter, expressing the wild spirits of the underworld.

Meanwhile, on the Dome, John Berwick paced up and down, a prey to conflicting motives. He was now full in the vortex of civil strife; a few short days and hostilities in all probability would open. He had no doubts now as to the spirit to be shown by the Police Commandant.

On Point Lookout sat Constable Hope, with his face towards the Upper Yukon. To the left he could see the Klondike Valley; to the right were the Police Barracks, with Dawson beyond them. His back was to the Dome. He sat still; a project was in his mind; he was thinking hard.

At the same time Smoothbore was in his office with Hi-u Bill, the Commissioner, and Inspector Herbert. Sergeant Galbraith stood at attention before them.

"You have ordered your men to be in readiness to fall back upon the Barracks. The orders for additional commissariat are placed with the different companies? The men, I suppose, pretty well understand what is in the wind?"

"Yes, sir," Galbraith answered to every question.

"And the men are in good spirits?"

"I have told them, sir, you intend to fight."

"And how do they seem to take it?"

"One of the fellows said he'd go to hell for you, sir."

"Well, that would seem satisfactory." The Commandant smiled grimly. "Our best hope is dissension among the rebels, and I have no idea how that may be brought about. That will do, Sergeant."

After the policeman had left there was silence for some time, which was at last broken by Hi-u Bill.

"I don't fancy they will do anything to me, and as I'm not called upon to fight I'm out of it. I am—and I suppose I may say it in modesty—a bit of a shot; but one has others to consider as well as himself."

The Commissioner was in the habit of spending his afternoons at target practice, which was not altogether appreciated by those whose business with him was pressing.

"I'm afraid you are altogether too modest; you know you're a famous shot."

Under usual circumstances Hi-u Bill was quite ready to receive compliments on his shooting, but the present circumstances were extraordinary, and he was undoubtedly perturbed. But the Commandant was merciless, for he continued,

"Of course, I am letting it be understood that I shall welcome all volunteers who desire to lend their aid at the present crisis."

"Yes, yes; no doubt there will be many who will avail themselves of the opportunity." Hi-u Bill was not over enthusiastic as he said this.

"Indeed, I think I could make my friends fairly comfortable under the circumstances."

"Certainly, quite so. My cabin at the North End is quite comfortable, and so close under the Dome that they could not shoot at me unless they came half-way down, in which case they would expose themselves to your fire. Capital idea that of yours, securing the long range sporting rifles. I almost feel sorry that I could not be with you here, as well as at my cabin, just to try a shot or two; but you see I think I had better stay outside. I have many friends among the old-timers, and nobody has ever accused me of doing anything serious. I certainly am not rich on ill-gotten gains." Hi-u Bill rubbed his hands nervously and cast a look at the Dome.

"Of course if you feel" — Smoothbore was choosing his words — "there is fear of any of the unsuccessful attributing their failure to you and wreaking vengeance on you I shall be quite happy to give you our protection."

"Oh, no, no. I prefer to run my chances outside; really I do."

Herbert, who was distressed equally at the irony of his Chief and the determined density of the Commissioner, diverted the conversation to another channel.

"In case of a siege, sir, there will be the question of water supply."

"Yes, I have thought of that. We shall have a supply from the river before hostilities break out, and after that a well may be sunk in twenty-four hours; the earth is not frozen here. But then if something turns up — —"

"Something turns up!" ejaculated Hi-u Bill, almost rising from his seat. "What could turn up? It would take an army eighteen months to get here across country, even by the Stikeen route; it will be close upon winter by the time news of this reaches Ottawa, and by the earliest time a force could be fitted out the Passes would be oceans deep in snow."

"I know—there's the luck of the British Empire!" There was a quiet smile on Smoothbore's lips. "Something always has turned up to save the British—except, except in the case of Gordon. That was the exception to the rule."

There was a sharp knock at the door, and the "Come in" was answered by Constable Hope—his face flushed. He was evidently very excited. The idea—on which for long he had been brooding—had come to maturity!

"I have a plan, sir, which will save us, I think. To carry it out I shall require gold, within limits, but the more the better."

Gold! The Commandant should have large quantities, the proceeds of royalty collections. Hi-u Bill pricked up his ears, bethought him of the fact, and asked directly,

"What have you done with all your gold?"

"I've had it buried. The plan of the exact spot will reach the authorities if we go under. But Forty Mile royalty came in to-day and has not yet been buried. How much do you want?" he asked. Constable Hope's heart gave a great leap as he realized he was going to be trusted.

"At least twenty thousand dollars, sir. Down River gold will do."

"Your plan will take that much?"

"I shall need that much, sir, but shall return it all, or nearly all."

"Very good, here it is." With the words the Commandant took a bag of gold out of a rough chest and handed it to the policeman.

"Thank you, sir, I——"

"That will do, Hope."

"Very good, sir." With the best salute he was master of the youth left the office.

Hi-u Bill had both eyes wide open, staring at Smoothbore. "What the devil——"

"That is just a tribute to the gods; I may not bribe our enemies, but the fates——"

"A bag of gold you can hardly lift! Why, your man will go down the River and stay down. You know the Yanks would afford him every protection, seeing that he stole from our Government."

"He won't steal the gold," replied Smoothbore.

"He won't! How do you know he won't?"

"I know my men!"

An unusual thing had happened. For a private to ask his Commanding Officer for the loan of twenty thousand dollars in gold, for that Commanding Officer to entrust it to him for some unexpressed purpose was strange—but many strange things happen on the frontier, and this was a time of crisis.

CHAPTER XXXIV
NO SURRENDER

Berwick's muster had been fifteen hundred strong on the Friday at noon. Of discipline there was little or none, and Berwick knew better than to attempt to enforce any. They had chosen him as their leader, and up to the present had not disputed his authority.

His directions were that the men should hold the Dome, retire to their camps in the forest to cook their food, but be ever-ready promptly to regain their position.

At noon he stood upon a boulder, and read to his followers the summons to surrender he had dispatched to Smoothbore. To the present— nine o'clock in the evening—no answer had been received, the summons to surrender was being received with contempt. He felt the responsibility upon him greater than ever; its weight increased as the time for the use of force approached. The twenty-four hours' notice before striking had nearly expired. He loathed the prospect of taking life, and prayed that the police would submit! If only they would see the hopelessness of resistance and send a pacific answer! Would that answer never come?

As he sat in meditation Berwick observed a restlessness among some men who were grouped, talking, gazing down the river. He looked in the same direction, and noticed a column of smoke. Then the hulk of a river steamer hove in sight. This visibly affected the men, who began to leave their posts and scramble down the hill to the town.

The arrival of a steamer in Dawson in the summer of 1898 was a matter of moment. An idea came to Berwick at the sight of her and the procession of people hurrying to meet her. He would go to the town. Everybody there would be keen to attend the docking of the steamer, making it practically certain that his visit to the Barracks would not be noticed. So to the Barracks he went.

"I wish to see the Officer commanding," he said to the sentry.

"Name?"

"John Berwick."

The man gulped, and stared at the visitor. He knocked at the door, and announced,

"A man to see you, sir, by name of John Berwick."

Hi-u Bill was again in the office, had just read the ultimatum, the discussion of which had been interrupted by the entrance of the man. He opened his eyes wide at the mention of the rebel's name.

"Show him in!"

Had the usual happy accident come to pass? flashed through Smoothbore's mind as he gazed with eyes of curiosity at the pseudo-President of the Klondike Free State that was to be.

Berwick entered, and stood facing the two chief executive officers of the Government. He at once picked out the Police Commandant, and returned his gaze without flinching.

"What can I do for you?" he was asked.

"I've come in the hopes of saving life. I have come to plead with you to comply with our request and surrender to our forces."

Smoothbore was struck by the transparent candour of the man and his quixotism. "British garrisons are not in the habit of surrendering at the call of rebels," he answered stiffly.

The word "rebel" roused Berwick. It stung. "I do not come to you from any cowardice, or through fear of death, or defeat. I come in the spirit of humanity."

"A very worthy mission! Then why not disband your forces?"

Berwick brushed the suggestion aside. "I have ten men for every one of yours, and my position commands these buildings. My men are in earnest, and there is justice in our cause, even to warrant the shedding of blood. This you must recognize."

"I recognize nothing but that I am here to uphold the law of the land."

"You must know—you must recognize—that great dishonesty exists within the Civil Service, and that we have met to protest and put an end to it!"

"Officially, I know nothing of that. It is my duty to maintain the Union Jack flying in the land."

"We can fire your buildings——"

"You may be able to fire our buildings; you may be able to kill us all; and then you may lower the flag. I tell you I intend to sink with my ship.

When you have burned us out, those men of mine—who wish to—may take to the river. That is all. You have my answer."

Berwick's eyes filled; a lump was in his throat. He gulped, and with a husky "Good-evening!" staggered into the open. He bent his head that the sentry might not see his emotion, and so gained the street by the Yukon's bank.

"He does not look much like a traitor," remarked Hi-u Bill.

"He is a man of evident ability. I fancy in England, in other days, he would have been a Whig. He has too little philosophy, or too much. Well, Commissioner," he said to Hi-u Bill, "are you going to stay with me, or run your chances in the town?"

"Me! I really think I'd better stay in my cabin. You see I am really not in this, and there are a lot of papers and records I had better bury somewhere."

On leaving the Barracks Berwick had been in somewhat of a daze. He was still in that condition when he found himself at the dock. The steamer *Susan* was tying to the wharf; the swift current had made docking difficult, so that he was in time to witness the landing of the passengers.

The crowd on the steamer was much as he had expected; but there was one man coming down the gang-plank who attracted his attention, and that of the onlookers generally; his hair fell to his shoulders; he had a great beard; his clothes were covered with grease, and he was very dirty.

He had a small pack strapped to his back; it was a very small pack—not much larger than a turnip; yet the figure that carried it bent under the load.

CHAPTER XXXV
THE MAN WITH THE POUCH

There were no signs of hesitancy in the movements of the man with the small round burden. He entered the Borealis, advanced to the bar, upon which he threw down the sack.

"Pass along your poison," said he to the bartender.

"What will it be?"

"What will it be! Why wine, what else would it be? Pass along a bottle."

"Large or small?"

"Large or small! Why large, of course! Say, son, what do you take me for?"

The bottle of wine was opened, and the new-comer quenched a willing thirst. He then turned to the crowd that had by this time clustered round him.

"Come on and have a drink, boys," he said, waving the bottle. "Belly-up to this good American timber." He jumped upon the bar and drank again. "Wine, wine! Give them wine, feed the nectar of the gods to the swine! Make 'em happy for once."

Notwithstanding the manner of the invitation, the crowd responded, and soon the two bartenders were busy.

"Stack the empties there so I can see and count 'em; thirty dollars per," and the host pointed to a shelf against the wall.

"Where did you get it?" shouted one of his guests.

He made no reply, but continued his tirade.

"Oh, you malamoots, you coyotes! You swine, descended of jackals! Drink, damn you, drink—you who live in this neck of the woods, and lie down and are robbed! no self-respecting jackal would own you for his sons. You who call yourselves citizens of the great and glorious United States! You're here rottin' in your cabins, the manhood squashed out of you by the yellow-legs. Say! throw the booze into you, and then tell me what I can call you to let you know how low down I think you."

"Say! partner," called another, "cut out all that and tell us where you got the swag."

"You sundowners and larrikins! Do you not remember Hanson's reward? Why don't you get in and dig?"

"Blow that, and tell us what's what—straight wire." Kalgoorlie Charlie also was feeling the effect of the liquor.

The man on the bar began to dance a hornpipe, while the crowd surged excitedly around. The news had spread like wildfire through the dance halls. "Some fellow from new diggings was blowing himself!" The Borealis soon became crowded.

"Oh, you lily-livered gelatinous-vertibraed apologies for men!" cried he. "What do you take me for? Me to go off into the bush for months and rustle new diggings, and then tell a lot of perambulating carrion like you where I struck it! Drink, and be damned to you! I don't care for a little gold. I wouldn't mind letting you have a claim next to mine; the claim I have will produce enough gold to make the Bank of England look like the baby's savings-account! Do you think I would show a bunch of Weary Willies like you where a month's work would make you all millionaires? Come, have another drink, and get wise."

The speaker again put the mouth of his bottle to his lips; but a keen observer would have noticed that his throat gave no movement to indicate that the wine was passing to his stomach. This was noticed by Berwick alone, who had followed the man with the big poke, but had stood just inside the doorway. Berwick guessed he was acting a part, and wondered why. He watched.

There was a confused buzz of conversation.

"He must have struck the real stuff," remarked one.

"He sure has the goods," agreed another.

"This will make a hole in his poke," said a third.

"If what he says is anything near right, this ain't a pinch of snuff," was the comment of a fourth.

The man dancing on the bar stood waving his bottle, looking at the crowd with a stupid stare, evidently awaiting inspiration, when a voice cried,

"Say! old cock, won't you let us have the news? We'll protect you in discovery."

"Oh, you North American Chinamen, called Canadians, do you know what I think of you? You English, you ain't no better than the others; do you all know what I think of you?"

"You've told us straight enough—there's lot's of colour in your bouquets; now tell us which way the new diggings is."

"There ain't no yellow-legs there."

Some one shouted, "There won't be any yellow-legs here after to-morrow," but the remark was lost in the general noise.

"It's in Alaskie—God's country," came a voice from the tumult.

"I did not say so."

"But it is, it is!"

"I don't say it ain't."

"It's in God's country—whereabouts?"

"That's what I ain't tellin'."

There was a clamour of inquiries. The new-comer, still holding his bottle prominently, was the target of eager gaze.

"Up the Porcupine—the Tanana, or the Koyukuck?"

"You must think I'm easy!" He spoke with a leer.

"You've made your stake, why not tell us where to make ours? It's a law of the frontier."

"So it is among pards. You ain't no pards of mine; I'm just standing you a few drinks out of pity, finding my reward in tellin' you what I think of you."

"You've told us what you think of us. Now tell us what we want to hear."

"Quite sure I've expressed myself strong enough?"

"Quite! Oh, quite!"—came from a dozen voices.

"Well, then, I'll tell you."

But he from the newly-found Eldorado stopped at the promise, and paused, regarding his audience. A strange silence came over the erstwhile struggling and swaying mass. The building was full, and the crowd extended into the street, where there were hundreds more; and to this great number additions were continually being made.

"Well, where is it?"

"It's on the south fork." The speaker put the bottle to his mouth once more.

Groans and hisses broke from the crowd. "If you don't tell us after keeping us here we'll string you up on a telegraph-pole."

"I did not keep you here: it was the free booze; besides, there ain't no telegraph-poles in Dawson."

"Well—we'll chuck you into the river."

"I'll swim out: I'm strong on baths—though perhaps I don't look it! Have another drink?"

"What we want now is a straight tip—and you had better give it."

"It's on the south fork of the north branch."

"The north branch of what?"

"I ain't tellin'."

"By God, you'd better! We ain't going to stand for more foolin'."

"You are all what I say you are—the scum of the earth."

"All right! We're anything you like: but let us have the news."

"It's the south fork of the north branch of the south fork——"

"What are you quitting for? why don't you spit it out of you?"

"Ain't I getting rid of it?"

"Not fast enough; quick, out with it!"

"Don't be impatient, sons, patience is a great virtue. It's taken me nigh to fifty years' hard prospecting to make a strike—and you fellows want me to tell you all about it in fifty minutes! How many minutes are there in fifty years?"

"You old fool, you'd better quit playing with us."

"Who wants to play with you?"

"You're teasing us; now quit! What river is this where you found the gold?"

"Well, it's the south fork of the north branch of the south fork of the south branch——"

"Oh, hell!" interrupted one of the impatient ones.

"There now, just when I get going you fellows spoil it all. Remember, it took fifty years almost——"

"And it will take you fifty years to tell us where you did find it."

"No, it won't; it's on the Fifty-Seven Mile River."

"The Fifty-Seven Mile River! The south fork of the north branch of the south fork of the north branch of the Fifty-Seven Mile River!" A great shout went up.

The Fifty-Seven Mile River emptied into the Yukon on the Canadian side, but it "headed" in Alaska, where the diggings probably were. Within two minutes the Borealis was practically empty.

Of the few remaining John Berwick was one. He stood with his back to the wall, staring at the man who still stood on the bar, who returned the stare. Meanwhile the host had turned to the row of bottles and begun the counting. The number was sixty. "Sixty! eighteen hundred dollars, cheap at double the money," said the man, who proceeded to weigh out the cost. That done he stalked out of the saloon and rapidly went his way. There was so much activity and excitement about that his progress to the Barracks was uninterrupted. No sooner was he within the gate than he tore off his beard and wig. It was Constable Hope.

Berwick had followed him from the saloon and watched him enter the Barracks. He now realized all that it meant. A blow had been struck at his organization. He realized that it was too late for any counter-effort. Greed of gold had taken possession of the men. A new rush was beginning. What call could reason, loyalty, righteousness make against that?

He wandered to the water-front and watched the activity, for within half an hour of the news of the supposed new strike being received boats had begun to shoot out from the river bank, bearing adventurers to the new diggings.

CHAPTER XXXVI
AFTER THE CRISIS

Mankind in Dawson having muddled its affairs, the gods took a hand in the game.

John Berwick, as he turned his face homewards early on the following day, happened to take the route that would carry him by the Barracks, notwithstanding that it would add a mile to the journey. As he climbed the hog's-back to Lookout Point he saw the tall military figure of Smoothbore in front of him. The Commandant, seeing him coming, awaited him.

"Good-morning. The air is very good."

"It is, indeed."

After this there was a pause. Evidently Smoothbore desired to make no reference to the interview of the preceding day. Possibly he judged the cause of the reformers to be already lost. If so Berwick would give him every opportunity of keeping the conversation from politics: so he continued,

"How pure the Klondike is and clear, and how beautiful are the shades across the Yukon!"

"'And only man is vile,'" quoted the Commandant.

Berwick realized that the Head of the Police was poking fun at him; and not knowing Smoothbore very well, concluded that he must know of the new stampede; in fact, he seemed to be watching the dark specks of moving men streaming over the summit of the Dome.

"Do you often walk abroad so early?" John asked.

"Yes, it is becoming a habit. One requires but little sleep in this climate; I shall soon return, and go to work."

"Are your labours heavy?"

"Oh, heavy enough; there are many details."

"You have a splendid force, sir."

"I have, and they are loyal to me and their country."

"Loyalty is among the chief of human virtues. But is loyalty in all cases a virtue?"

"I consider it so."

"Your men must find many duties distasteful to them."

"Duty is often distasteful, but it is never to be mistaken. With me it is very well defined. Are you also taking a morning constitutional?"

"I am going up to the Dome." It would not do for John to let the other know the whereabouts of his abode or to divulge the fact that it was his custom to sleep at night. It was a custom with many in that city of perpetual light to sleep in the normal daytime and work at night.

"I'm going the same way. We'll walk together. I wish to spy out the land a bit. We may decide to build a trail to Moosehide."

The two continued on the winding trail, which was now lined with human habitations, set down without any idea of system. Some were cabins, others tents, others still a combination of the two—such, indeed, as was John's "home-ranch." Before many of them camp-fires were crackling and burning, and meals were being prepared. The two who were or had been the leaders of the opposing parties passed without attention being paid to them.

"Ah! there's the danger signal, the result of the first frost, and a sign that summer will soon pass away." John pointed to a willow whose leaves had turned crimson and scarlet.

"Yes, we shall have winter soon; this weather won't last. But you are in error in supposing that the bright tints in our foliage are due to frost; the mistake is very common. The redness is mere ripeness."

They found many topics in common, and mutual interest made the stiff effort less trying as they climbed and climbed.

As they approached a point on the trail, half way to the summit, a man was seen coming down, dragging a log by a rope. They stepped aside from the path, which here was on the side hill. Berwick, who was outside, happened to place his foot on a loose lump of moss lying on a stone. It moved; his foot slipped; he lost his balance. He struggled on the shelving ground, grabbed at some grass, was tangled in some brush, tore his hands, went down with a crash, being stopped by a sharpened stump of a severed tree-trunk. The point grazed his arm and pierced the body under the shoulder-blade. At once the Commandant and the woodman went to his help, but the jar of attempting to raise him brought a cry of pain. It was necessary to cut the tree-stump before he could be assisted to his feet.

They had to carry him down the hill, his mind in a half-swoon punctuated with throbs and stabs of pain, until he awoke to consciousness in the St. George's Hospital.

It seemed more as the remembrance of a dream than of actual occurrence. He was in England. Even the voice of Alice ...

A pungent odour was about him. He heard a buzzing rising rapidly in key, higher—higher—yet higher; higher—higher still; then there was a "click." As John Berwick's senses were stolen away by the blessed influence of an anæsthetic his lips framed the word "Alice." She heard the name, and was glad.

The first words John uttered as the drug left him were incoherent; but gradually they took form.

"Who's afraid to die? I'm not afraid to die. What's the good of a man's religion if he's afraid to die?"

"I know you're not afraid to die," said Alice.

The only reply she got was, "Oh, my head! my head!"

"What's the matter with your head?"

"Oh, my head! it's bursting."

"Water! water!" continued to be his cry; but Alice would feed him with only a drop or two at a time. Gradually his ravings grew less pronounced, less frequent.

"Who are you?" he asked, after gazing for some time with dazed eyes at Alice. "You look very like Alice Peel. Alice is in England, and I am—where am I?"

"I'm glad I look like Alice Peel," she said in reply.

"She's the only girl—in all the world," he murmured, before his mind again wandered, and he muttered straggling fragments of verses.

"Alice, Alice!" he cried suddenly.

"Yes," said Alice, soothing his head with her cool hand.

He recognized her. "Alice!" he cried again.

She bent over and kissed him. "Go to sleep," she said.

John did as he was commanded. When he woke two hours later he called for water, and Alice gave him some from a cup.

"Alice, I've been wounded; yes, I remember that—but how did you get here?"

"I will tell you to-morrow when you are stronger. You must not excite yourself now."

But at six o'clock that evening Surgeon-Major Peel, taking his temperature and finding it normal, gave the necessary permission. So Alice told their story.

CHAPTER XXXVII
OIL ON TROUBLED WATERS

John Berwick's accident was the last touch which caused the uprising to crumble. One more great effort after the ideal of justice had fallen and parted.

Frank Corte was sitting in front of the Dominion Creek cabin, by the side of a pool of water that had formed since the claims—which rightfully belonged to himself and his three associates—had been taken over by the agents of Poo-Bah. The policy of the land was to reap to-day and spend to-morrow, so a dam had been put in on the "pup" or tributary of Dominion Creek that entered above the claims; and already a harvest was in sight. Frank had some possessions in the cabin, which he had come to fetch before joining the new stampede.

Above the cabin was a line of sluice-boxes, into which half-a-dozen lusty Scandinavians were shovelling the precious dirt. It was Frank's own claim they were working—and he gritted his teeth. For an instant his face lost its habitual grin. "If this was only God's country," he muttered, as he glanced through the open door of the cabin at the rifle hanging on the wall therein. He continued to whirl the gold-pan which he held in his hands. In the pan was a handful of dirt he was idly concentrating. "The boss won't stand for it—and he's a white man." Frank smiled again.

From the mining operations at the sluice-boxes, voices came to where Corte sat. Neither the foreman nor his men had realized that their voices were carrying beyond the sound of rushing water. They were shouting that they might hear each other above the roar in the sluices, and were laughing cheerily—for Poo-Bah was a good paymaster to his men. "One dollar, two dollar, one and six bits"—would float to Frank's ears, as the foreman estimated the contents of a pan; and he would inwardly groan as he calculated the wealth that was passing from him into the great grafter's pocket.

"I guess we'd better clean up; we can get her down to the black sand by half-past ten and finished an hour later."

Something rose in Frank's throat and almost choked him. The attitude of these intruders galled him. He half jumped up to seize his rifle, when "No," he muttered: "Them yellow-legs!"

His attention was attracted to the gold-pan. Specks of gold were floating upon the water; at the bottom of the pan he noticed an unmistakable grease spot, and, true to its nature, it had secured to its surface several of the tiny yellow grains. Grease was alike fatal to the gold-pan and the stamp battery.

Suddenly his eyes took on a new light: they were full of energy. He glanced towards the working miners, and followed the line of sluices to the artificial pond in the "pup" whence they got their water. "Yes, yes!" he muttered, and sprang to his feet. He hurried to the quarters of one of his friends, Jerry, the engineer on a neighbouring claim where a steam-plant had been installed.

"Jerry," said Frank, "I want two bottles of lubricating oil."

"Pretty near all I got."

"Don't care—must have it."

"All right, what do you want it for?"

"Frying slap-jacks." Frank went with his evil-smelling petroleum.

"What the devil is he up to!" asked Jerry, as the drooping figure hulked out of sight. The weasel that peeped at him through the poles of his cabin floor could not tell him, nor did he know.

Frank put the oil on the table of his cabin, and then went outside and began chopping wood. It was now the orthodox bed-time, so he must show a good reason for being about. The sun had just set in the north, the quarter it sets in the Northland.

"Shut her off," he heard the foreman cry, and he knew the cleaning was to be commenced. Down came the axe on a four-inch stick of spruce with a force that burst it asunder and threw the pieces far apart. No experienced woodman in the ordinary course of events would have used so much force, and Frank Corte had chopped much wood.

The roar of the water diminished, the voices of the clean-up men fell away. He could hear no more, but he knew every move. First, the riffles would be lifted from the sluice-boxes and the dump-box, and the dirt in the sluice-boxes would be shovelled into the dump-box. Then a strip of wood, about two inches square, would be placed across the dump-box where it joined the head of the sluices. This would prevent the gold from being washed down the boxes.

When these processes were accomplished the foreman shouted "Turn on half a head," and Ole Oleson, at the gate, allowed half the usual flow of water to rush down the flume to the dump-box. Had Frank watched the impact of the water on the dirt in the dump-box he would, even in the now failing light, have seen a burst of yellow shine out from what had previously appeared dross.

As the water reached the dirt the dirt was forced against it by three or four stout paddles, whereby the husky workmen churned and washed the dirt thoroughly. Across the dump-box where the water met the pay-dirt stretched a band of gold. First it was half an inch, and then two inches. Meanwhile the pebbles and the dross worked their way over the retaining block and bumped ignominiously to the tailings.

"It looks good," said the foreman in loud tones. Frank heard him then shout to Ole, "A quarter of a head." Corte, thereupon, threw down his axe. It was time for action. He went into the cabin, and placed the two bottles of oil in a bucket, with which he set out for the dam. It was the most natural thing in the world for a man to draw a bucket of water before retiring: he might want a drink during the night.

Ole was almost asleep when Frank came up to him. He was lounging over the gate. Frank greeted him with, "Good-evening, partner; you're working late to-night."

"Dat's so," was all Ole had life enough to answer. Frank slipped his bucket into the water; the bottle sank against the mud. The hues of iridescence spread across the weird and silent surface.

The bottles were safely at the bottom of the pool, and the bucket full of water, as Frank turned towards the cabin, saying, "Good-night, Ole." As he neared his cabin he heard the foreman shout, "Shut her half off"; and knew that the work of taking out the black sand from the dust was at hand. He knew that already the small specks of gold were being carried to the lower end of the pool. So he made haste, and, taking a blanket, nailed it at the waste gate of the lower pond, so that the total flood from above went through it: then he turned in.

He was awake at four on the next morning, and, proceeding to the lower pond, loosed the blanket, which was heavy with water and gold. Then he built a fire in the open, and after it was burning well placed the blanket upon it.

When the blanket was totally consumed and the fire burnt down, Frank collected the ashes and panned them out. The gold was fine in form and quality, and proved worth some thousands of dollars.

"Hi-u chickaman stuff," laughed Frank.

CHAPTER XXXVIII
REUNION

Frank Corte, "mushing" through to Dawson from Dominion Creek, took his time comfortably and arrived on the second evening. He danced till five in the morning, after which, as was natural, he lay down and slept. Accordingly it was not until the evening after his arrival that he gave a thought to his three companions, and began to search for them by visiting the Borealis, and going the round of the dance-halls and gambling-saloons. He found George and Hugh, who were together, but not John.

Something must surely have happened to him! George Bruce had visited his den several times lately; he was not there. At last by inquiry at the police station they learnt that he had hurt himself by falling when climbing to the Dome, and had been taken to St. George's Private Hospital.

It was about nine in the evening when the three friends visited him in the ward.

"Hello, what's wrong now?" Frank cried; "better than typhoid anyway."

Alice rose in indignation at the noise and clatter; but seeing John smile, reseated herself. Frank was broadly grinning.

"Alice, this is Frank Corte, my good friend, George Bruce and Hugh Spencer, my pards; now you know personally the good fellows I've told you about."

Alice shook hands with them, and there was a moment of some awkwardness, which Frank broke by saying, "Here," as he laid a large poke of gold on John's chest.

"Where did you get it?" asked he.

Frank took a sly glance at Alice — in fact, he had already taken several. She was certainly attractive, and had impressed him. His usual vocabulary was insufficient in the circumstances. He gave a sniff.

"I applicationed the principles of childish lore to the exigencies of existence in a land of graft and corruption; I lubricated the wheels of the flow of justice and distracted this here gold-dust from Poo-Bah."

"Who?" inquired Alice, frankly laughing.

"Poo-Bah—he's the high mucky-muck round here, sort of 'man Friday' to the Octopus who's got his tentacles round these here environs."

"How did you get the dust?" asked John again, as with critical eyes he estimated the value of the contents of the poke.

"Well, I was sitting in front of our cabin on the claims with my brain working and my eyes on the 'quivi-vivi,' as them Frenchers would say, and I was ebolluting hot, and then I thought of grease! So I gets some lubricating oil, and then Nature does the rest; of course I was the instrument whereby the oil was placed in the sluices."

John grasped Frank's meaning and method. It flashed upon him at the mention of the lubricating oil.

"What do you mean to do with this gold?" Berwick asked.

"You are going to keep it."

"Oh, no, I can't do that; why give it to me? Why to me more than to Hugh?"

"Oh, he can get more. He's coming with me to God's country."

"Where?" asked Alice, more than ever bewildered.

"To God's country—the new strike down in Alaska; there'll be no Poo-Bah there, and plenty of shot-gun justice."

"But there's George's interest."

"George! Oh, he will put his up with ours O.K., I guess." Here Frank again looked at Alice. "I guess you'll be needing that stuff if parsons charge like other folks do!"

John smiled at this, and Alice blushed. Leaving the friends together, for she knew they would wish to talk, she went from the room.

"No, no, Frank, it won't do." Then, seeing that Corte looked troubled, he added, "I'll take a quarter if you like; you've proved yourself a comrade. But what's this about the new strike?"

"Big gold excitement—richer than Bonanza and Eldorado, and, best of all, in God's country; you'll be coming?"

"I—no, you must remember my work. Are you for giving up our enterprise to get justice done here and in other goldfields?"

"Sure thing, me and Hugh, in fact, everything that don't wear hobbles is going."

"And leave all this wrong unrighted?"

"Sure thing; this ain't my country. I'm going where things can be made right overnight, and there ain't no yellow-legs."

"And you, Hugh, are you going to Alaska?"

"Yes, I think so; you see the chances of getting in on a new strike seem good—and—well, our great show has melted right away. It was a fine effort, but it failed. I don't mind running chances—in fact, I'm used to it; and, after all, that's all Poo-Bah and his chums know, is grafting. Let them keep their dirty money."

"It's a pity, a pity." John was thoughtful for a time. They were looking at him. "I don't know what I shall do if you and Frank desert me," sighed John.

"Get married and settle down," Frank said bluntly.

"You'll do all right," interposed Hugh, "you and George got record for two claims on the left limit of Bonanza working out your quartz proposition right against discovery. Well, this is Chechacho Hill, now reckoned amongst the richest ground in all the Klondike. You and George don't need to worry about Poo-Bah and Dominion Creek hillsides, nor your daily bread, no more. I thought I would not tell George the news till I caught you two together. Frank and I will try our chances again, and George can stay here and watch you 'live happy ever afterwards.'"

John frowned; his mind reverted to his "Mission." He believed that his duty was to the great portion of the Klondike's population whom Poo-Bah and the system of grafters had wronged. He refused even yet to recognize the game was up.

"Our people——" he began.

"Our people are mostly down the river striking for God's country, where there ain't no yellow-legs, and a shot-gun holds down your claim!"

"Frank is right," interposed Hugh, "our whole big following has gone."

John knew this to be only too true. Alas! alas! the fickleness of man.

"Just like the Siwash, Si-Ya Creeks, Hi-u Chickaman, we're all much alike, yes—yes, except some"—and Frank glanced at Alice, who then entered the room with refreshment for the visitors.

"Frank says that far-away creeks appear to hold much gold," John translated for the benefit of Alice.

"Well, you're all right with your gold on Chechacho Hill," said Hugh. "I might have known it was there if I had only thought."

"Why?" asked Bruce.

"Because of Carmack finding gold on top of twenty feet of muck. I might have known that the gold slid down the hill. It wasn't creek gold Bonanza was discovered on—no, sir, it was hillside. And that accounts for its being above the muck there and nowhere else. If a fellow could only think right before he knows!"

"We'll try and know right down in God's country, Boss. Hugh and I must be going now. George won't be going with us; he has his claim in this yellow-leg country."

In the way of the goldfields, they proceeded at once to say good-bye. Corte and Spencer took their shares of the gold Frank had brought from Dominion Creek, and went, carrying all manner of wishes for good from those they were leaving behind.

CHAPTER XXXIX
RETROSPECTION

Constable Hope had been attracted by John Berwick, and meant to see more of him. So that when he met him one day with his arm in a sling he showed himself friendly.

Smoothbore's trooper was a youth of ideas—a good type of the fine force. Though he was still but twenty-four years of age his life had so often been in danger that he had courage and character far beyond his years. As the incident which broke down the conspiracy had proved, he was an adventurer at heart, with more than usual brilliance and spirit.

He would ride into a band of yelling drunken savages and get his man without showing a gun, and time and again had solved difficulties through sheer daring, cleverness, and shrewd knowledge of men. He played the game for love of the game. Money, by way of graft, he did not deem any reward.

John Berwick had interested him. He felt that they held interests in common, so when they met he addressed him. He was not in uniform, and Berwick had no idea he belonged to the police.

He followed John into one of the gambling-halls, whither John had gone in search of any of his old-time colleagues who might not have joined the stampede.

As, standing beside each other, they watched the play at a Black Jack table, a burly Swede lounged up, and from his hip pocket drew out a bag of dust, which he laid on the table in line with the wagers of the other players. The sack held about three thousand dollars-worth of gold.

The dealer dealt each man a card, slipping it under his wager, and then dealt another round. The different players, starting with the one on the dealer's left, after looking at what they had drawn, either tapped their cards if they wished another card or placed their hand beneath their wager if they were content to "stand."

When it came to the Scandinavian's turn he stood stupidly looking at his gold.

"Well—what do you intend to do?" asked the dealer.

"Have I got to leave that gold there?"

"No, you can take it up if you want to," replied the other.

The Swede hesitated, then picked up his gold and walked away, while the dealer idly turned over the cards, at sight of which even the stoic Dawson audience grew noisy with comments. The cards turned up were an ace and a king—Black Jack, a winning hand against all others.

"That's what a fellow gets whose nerve fails him," remarked Constable Hope.

"Yes, but perhaps it is not always better to win."

Constable Hope glanced shrewdly at John. He followed up the thought with a searching remark.

"I wonder if it would have been better if the miners had won against the officials."

"I wonder!" The remark was not encouraging.

"I heard you make your speech at the finish of the Dominion Creek stampede," Hope persisted in saying; "there does not seem to be much agitation in these days."

"No, the discontented, or rather the wronged, have gone down the river, preferring the chances of a new field to securing justice here. Those who have property are afraid to speak. A goldfield is not a place where principle flourishes."

"You're not like the Swede; you didn't lose your nerve," said Hope.

Berwick made no reply.

"Did you ever see a good man lose his nerve?" the policeman asked.

"No."

"Well, I have. Once I was in the mountains down below with a buck policeman, a Scotch-Canadian from back east, and as good a trooper as ever sat a horse. Got lost in a blizzard on the prairies later on, and they never found him till spring—the coyotes had not left much of him. Well, Chisholm and I went hunting one day, and, travelling along, came to a box canyon. We decided to try and cross it; it was a couple of hundred feet deep, and we started, Chisholm going first. I let him down, he holding my hands with one of his, while with the other he grabbed a bush. No sooner had he put his foot on the ledge we figured on getting down to than he found it soft and yielding. For some reason he dropped my hand and grabbed at a tuft of moss and hung there. Then his footing went further down, which drew his chest tight against the wall of the canyon. I threw myself on my stomach and grabbed him by the collar and said, 'Jump.' His eyes glistened, and he appeared not to hear me. Then I looked over the edge and saw that the ledge he had been standing on had given way entirely, and that he was suspended by his arms alone. He would not speak; he would not move. The wild light in his eyes faded a bit, but there he hung, to all appearance dead. Had I not had a lariat with me I should have been powerless. As it was, I got a slip-knot around his feet, and so up under his arms, and this I made fast to a tree. Then I laughed at him. It is a wonderful light, that which comes into men's eyes at the fear of death. I have only seen it once again—in the eyes of a mother travelling on a river steamer who thought her child had fallen overboard. Losing your nerve is dangerous."

When their drink and Hope's story were finished they walked out in the street, where they met Smoothbore. As they passed him John nodded, and his companion brought his hand half way to the salute and then lowered it. Hope had given himself away; the other saw he was a policeman.

"You know Smoothbore?" Hope asked.

"I have spoken to him."

Hope did not reply for a moment, after which he continued, "There's a man who never loses his nerve."

It was the highest tribute Hope could pay.

"Did you ever hear of Paper-collar Johnnie?"

"No," said John.

"Paper-collar was an officer down below, and he and Smoothbore were pals. They were out to a banquet one night and returning home late—in fact dawn was breaking over the prairie, cold and misty, when they reached the ford of the river outside their post. It had been raining hard, the stream had risen, and the driver drew up before the ford and said, 'The river seems pretty bad, sir.' 'Hold on,' said Paper-collar, 'this won't do; mustn't try and cross that ford if the river is in flood.' 'Driver, halt,' ordered Smoothbore, 'my companion wishes to alight; get down, sir.' Paper-collar stepped down on the prairie. 'Now, driver, the ford.'"

"And he took it all right?"

"Yes, sir; and hours afterwards a patrol from the fort picked up poor Paper-collar."

"What would Smoothbore have done had the miners risen after the Dominion Creek stampede?" Berwick ventured to ask.

"He'd have fought, and the police would have stood by him. He'd have used his nerve."

"I learn there is a 'Nordenfelt' and a maxim in the Passes. If the miners had got them down here and hauled them to the top of the Dome they would have made things hot in the Barracks."

"Well, maxim or no maxim, Smoothbore would have fought. Neither he nor any of the police do any grafting; but we should have fought."

"Perhaps it is as well the Alaska stampede began," said Berwick musingly.

"It was very much better," said Hope decisively. So they parted, and Berwick felt the last word had been said about his bid for miners' justice.

CHAPTER XL
THE HAPPY ENDING

When, the next day, Alice accompanied John and George Bruce in a first visit to their claims on Chechacho Hill, they saw that the signal thrown out by the first red tints of the maples and the willows—which told of summer ending and the dreary months of winter beginning—was shown. The sun was shining brightly, but already it seemed robbed of some of its heat.

Alice had often pictured life at the diggings. She had read numbers of mining-camp stories, with scenes laid in America and Australia, yet had gained little insight to the realities. She gloried in the experience, and was eager to urge them on. "Hurry! hurry!" but John exhorted her to stay her speed, for the distance they had to go was twenty-four miles, and the trail—though many of the mud-holes had dried—was rough.

She looked at the men she met, hunting for the type of her fancy, the type engendered by novel and tale. No one seemed armed, save occasionally with a rifle or a shot-gun; but the wild man with the brace of pistols, bandolier, huge moustache and homicidal aspect did not present himself!

They crossed the Klondike by Poo-Bah's ferry. Once in Bonanza Valley Alice felt she had left the civilized world behind her, and was entering the enchanted regions of Nature. To her, in her happy illusions, it was fairy-land.

Few women had preceded her over the Bonanza trail, so that men, "mushing," who passed their fellows with lowered head, openly stared at her; and many of these lonely wayfarers would have been glad of a word from her, to hear again the sweet soft accents of the better world outside. For to the men of the frontier the idea of home is very refined and dear, and women ever virtuous and tender, so that the appearance of Alice Peel, on the Bonanza trail upon that glorious day, was to them as a beautiful picture and an uplifting influence.

One grizzled miner hurried out, holding a gold-pan full of nuggets, dust, and black sand.

"Put your hand into it, lady, and see what it feels like."

Alice did so, and thought it felt like any other sand, only heavier. He then selected a nugget—worth quite a sovereign—from the pan and gave it to her.

"Why did you give me this?"

"Because you are a lady."

Alice looked perplexed.

"Keep it as a souvenir," said John, so she thanked the man and slipped the nugget inside her glove. But that was not to be the limit of their host's hospitality, for, as they turned to go, he said,

"It's just about noon, and if you've walked from Dawson the lady must be near petered. Better stay and have dinner."

"We thought of dining at the road-house at Discovery," said George. "We have some ground on Chechacho Hill."

"I can give you a better feed here: moose-meat, either steak or nose, whichever you fancy. You see, lady, in the old days this was a sort of a pet locality for moose, so they stray in once in a while yet, and sometimes they don't get a chance to get away again."

The sound of a horn came from a tent close by.

The signal was answered by a general throwing down of tools, and the half-dozen men at work made their way towards the tent. They all washed in a couple of tin basins, and dried themselves on a filthy towel.

Alice and her companions were ushered into the dining-tent, where, John's quick eyes noticed, extra places had been set. Alice was asked to sit at the head of the table, in the owner's place: John and George were seated at her right, and the owner—Wild Horse Bill—on the left. The men were already hard at work, consuming their food—moose-steak, pork and beans, and great pieces of bread.

As they sat down the cook placed on the table a large tin platter, in which was a piece of meat of indescribable colour and shape.

"This is moose nose, lady, the best part of the animal, and along with the beaver tail and wild-cat makes the finest eating in the Northland."

"Wild-cat!" Alice exclaimed. She had indeed read of the tail of Canada's mascot being a frontier dainty, but moose nose, and especially wild-cat, were new, and did not sound altogether attractive articles of diet.

"Yes, lady, the lynx, or wild-cat, is the best eating the trapper knows in the Northland. You would think you were eating chicken. As for moose nose and beaver tail, one is much like the other."

The owner pushed the platter containing the strange dainty towards Alice, with the words, "Help yourself, lady."

Alice was game; and, without showing her disinclination, she took up the knife and fork and cut off a piece of the blubberous meat, and put it on her plate.

After they had walked about a mile and a half beyond the claim where they had lunched they stood beneath Chechacho Hill at the northeast, a quarter of a mile down-stream from where Carmack had made his discovery; and John pointed to where their claims were situate. Men were at work, "rocking" gold on the next claim to John's.

When they reached their claims Alice looked across the valley, noting the great stretches of poplar and birch, golden-yellow in their autumn tints, and smiled at the beauty of it—till out of the chilled atmosphere somewhere came the whisper, "Make haste and provide."

"I should like to live here always," whispered Alice to John, while Bruce went to talk with the men working on the claim alongside.

"Always is a long time, and every day will not be as beautiful as this; but for a year or two——"

"Yes, for a year or two."

And so it was decided.

They were married in the little church by the side of the slough in Dawson.